Winter Wonderlands

The World's Best Christmas Markets

By
Sophie Antonia Merritt

Copyright 2024 Lars Meiertoberens. All rights reserved.

No part of this book may be reproduced in any form or by any electronic or mechanical means including information storage and retrieval systems, without permission in writing from the author. The only exception is by a reviewer, who may quote short excerpts in a review.

Although the author and publisher have made every effort to ensure that the information in this book was correct at press time, the author and publisher do not assume and hereby disclaim any liability to any party for any loss, damage, or disruption caused by errors or omissions, whether such errors or omissions result from negligence, accident, or any other cause.

This publication is designed to provide accurate and authoritative information with regard to the subject matter covered. It is sold with the understanding that the publisher is not engaged in rendering professional services. If legal advice or other expert assistance is required, the services of a competent professional should be sought.

The fact that an organization or website is referred to in this work as a citation and/or a potential source of further information does not mean that the author or the publisher endorses the information the organization or website may provide or recommendations it may make.

Please remember that Internet websites listed in this work may have changed or disappeared between when this work was written and when it is read.

Winter Wonderlands

The World's Best Christmas Markets

Table of Contents

Introduction 1

Chapter 1: The Magic of European Christmas Markets 4
    Germany's Holiday Heritage 4
    Austria's Winter Charm 9

Chapter 2: France's Enchanting Celebrations 13
    Strasbourg's Captivating Lights 13
    Paris's Holiday Elegance 17

Chapter 3: The United Kingdom's Festive Delights 20
    London's Winter Wonderland 20
    Edinburgh's Magical Markets 22

Chapter 4: The Nordic Yuletide Experience 26
    Sweden's Seasonal Splendor 26
    Finland's Snowy Celebrations 29

Chapter 5: Spain's Holiday Fervor 33
    Barcelona's Festive Flair 33
    Madrid's Merry Traditions 36

Chapter 6: Italy's Christmas Artistry 40
    Florence's Artisanal Wonders 40
    Rome's Religious and Festive Blend 43

Chapter 7: Switzerland's Alpine Markets 46
    Zurich's Christmas Markets 46
    Lucerne's Lakeside Charm 49

Chapter 8: Belgium's Winter Wonders 53
Brussels's Grand Place Magic 53
Bruges's Medieval Markets 55

Chapter 9: Eastern Europe's Yuletide Spirit 59
Prague's Holiday Enchantment 59
Budapest's Festive Warmth 62

Chapter 10: The Netherlands' Festive Glow 65
Amsterdam's Winter Fun 65
Maastricht's Magical Markets 68

Chapter 11: The Baltic Winter Celebrations 72
Tallinn's Timeless Traditions 72
Riga's Charming Stalls 75

Chapter 12: Russia's Winter Extravaganza 78
Moscow's Festive Squares 78
St. Petersburg's Snowy Delights 81

Chapter 13: The Danube Region's Seasonal Charm 85
Vienna to Bratislava's Twin Celebrations 85
Budapest's Riverside Markets 88

Chapter 14: Poland's Holiday Heritage 91
Krakow's Medieval Magic 91
Warsaw's Winter Wonderland 94

Chapter 15: The Balkan's Festive Spirit 97
Croatia's Coastal Celebrations 97
Serbia's Vibrant Traditions 100

Chapter 16: The Unique Allure of Eastern
Mediterranean Markets 104
Greece's Festive Fusion 104
Turkey's Cultural Blend 107

Chapter 17: Christmas in the United States 111

New York's Iconic Markets 111
Chicago's Festive Diversity 114

Chapter 18: Canada's Winter Marvels 117
Montreal's Joyful Festivities 117
Toronto's Holiday Lights 120

Chapter 19: South America's Holiday Celebrations 124
Brazil's Tropical Traditions 124
Argentina's Festive Blend 127

Chapter 20: Asia's Festive Fusion 131
Japan's Illuminated Celebrations 131
South Korea's Holiday Extravaganza 134

Chapter 21: Australia's Sunny Yuletide 138
Sydney's Unique Celebrations 138
Melbourne's Festive Traditions 141

Chapter 22: New Zealand's Seasonal Blend 145
Auckland's Antipodean Celebrations 145
Wellington's Windy Festivities 148

Chapter 23: Christmas Markets of the Middle East 152
Lebanon's Cultural Celebrations 152
Jordan's Festive Discoveries 155

Chapter 24: Africa's Unique Festive Traditions 158
South Africa's Sunlit Markets 158
Morocco's Cultural Blend 161

Chapter 25: Embracing Christmas Markets Around the Globe 165
Uniting Winter Festivals 165
Global Traditions and Modern Twists 168

Conclusion 172

Appendix A: Appendix 174

Introduction

The glow of twinkling lights, the scent of freshly baked gingerbread, and the joyous sound of carolers singing in the crisp winter air—these are the hallmarks of Christmas markets worldwide. Embarking on a journey to explore these markets isn't just a holiday trip; it's an immersion into a rich tapestry of cultural traditions and festive spirit. The allure of Christmas markets lies not only in their visual beauty but also in their ability to evoke a sense of wonder and nostalgia, enchanting travelers from near and far.

Christmas markets, known for their unique capacity to transform ordinary city squares into festive wonderlands, invite you to step into a realm where history and modernity blend seamlessly. These markets are as much about community and cultural heritage as they are about celebration. Each one, with its distinctive personality and charm, offers a glimpse into the local traditions and ways of life. From the quaint cobblestone paths of Europe to the contemporary settings in North America and beyond, every market tells its own story—a story wrapped in centuries of tradition.

At the heart of these markets lies the spirit of Christmas, a time for gathering, giving, and reflecting. As the world becomes increasingly digital, the tangible experience of wandering through a market, savoring local delicacies, and finding that perfect handcrafted gift is a treasured tradition that remains steadfast. In a globalized world, Christmas markets preserve the essence of locality, offering visitors a chance to support artisans and participate in age-old customs.

The diversity of Christmas markets around the globe is as vast as the cultures they represent. While European markets, with their medieval roots, often take center stage, festive scenes in Asia, the Americas, and beyond are gaining momentum. Adventurers find themselves at home amid the lights and laughter, discovering that the magic of Christmas transcends borders. These markets are more than attractions; they are living exhibitions of the world's eclectic holiday expressions.

Imagine strolling through a snow-dusted plaza, the aroma of mulled wine mingling with that of warm chestnuts roasting over an open fire. Vendors beckon with handcrafted ornaments, each piece telling its own story of craftsmanship and love. While visiting these markets, you're not just a tourist; you're part of a timeless tradition stretching back hundreds of years. With each step, you write yourself into the shared narrative of joyous gatherings and festive delight.

Whether nestled against the backdrop of majestic mountains, perched along winding riverbanks, or spread across bustling urban squares, Christmas markets bring a unique blend of spectacle and intimacy. Seasonal markets transform ordinary surroundings into enchanting destinations, becoming more magical at night when lights string across booths and trees, turning the scene into a luminous fairyland. It's an ambiance that captivates both the young and the old, creating lasting memories for families and solo travelers alike.

There's a profound joy in discovering the varying themes and offerings of each market, from the simplicity of wooden stalls adorned with evergreen boughs to grand visual spectacles featuring elaborate decorations. Some markets feature ice-skating rinks, while others boast towering Christmas trees or nativity scenes. Each city finds its own way to express the holiday spirit, drawing from a well of local mythology and regional flavors.

For many, the heart of the Christmas market lies in the communal experience. These markets provide a space for gathering and sharing stories, promoting an understanding of diverse customs and traditions. As you wander between stalls and sip on a hot beverage to ward off the winter chill, there's also a conversation happening—a dance between the past and the present. They invite travelers to embrace both the familiar and the new, to engage with the world in a way that is both introspective and outward-reaching.

While the market landscape may change from one destination to another, the unifying element of joy remains. It's a potent reminder of the true meaning of the season, one that inspires a sense of wonder and hope. Whether for a brief visit or a leisurely stroll, every moment spent at a Christmas market is an opportunity to reflect on the abundant beauty and shared humanity of this remarkable world we call home.

In these pages, we'll take you on a journey across continents, exploring the festive beauty and cultural treasures that await. We'll delve into the traditions that make each market unique, celebrating both time-honored practices and new interpretations. Along the way, we hope to spark your curiosity and inspire you to set out on your own adventure, experiencing firsthand the charm and delight of the world's most beloved holiday events.

As you turn the pages, allow yourself to be enveloped by the stories and visions of faraway places, yet familiar in their festive embrace. Let the imaginations of those who craft, those who celebrate, and those who wander illuminate your journey. Welcome to a world where every market is a heartwarming invitation to rediscover the magic of Christmas and to cherish the joyous connections that bind us all together.

Chapter 1:
The Magic of European Christmas Markets

Stepping into the heart of a European Christmas market is like walking into a scene from a fairytale, where centuries-old traditions twinkle under a canopy of festive lights. The air turns crisp, filled with the enticing aroma of gingerbread, mulled wine, and roasting chestnuts mingling with the distant echo of carolers. Each market—whether it's nestled in the bustling squares of Nuremberg or the elegant streets of Vienna—offers a unique tapestry of cultural heritage and holiday cheer. Stalls brimming with handcrafted ornaments and local delicacies invite travelers to immerse themselves in the season's magic. It's not just about the shopping; it's about experiencing a sense of community and warmth that transcends the frosty air. Here, in the enchanting glow of wooden chalets adorned with fresh pine and twinkling lights, one discovers the simple joys and timeless wonders that make Europe's Christmas markets a destination to cherish during the festive season.

Germany's Holiday Heritage

Germany stands as the quintessential heart of European Christmas tradition, blending history and festivity in a way that's become iconic worldwide. The country's holiday heritage is steeped in warm, time-honored traditions that have evolved into the magical experiences we treasure today. Strolling through a Christmas market here, you're enveloped in the glow of twinkling lights and the delightful scent of spiced mulled wine. These markets are more than just a feast for the senses; they're a window into a rich cultural legacy. Picture yourself wandering past quaint wooden stalls adorned with handcrafted ornaments, each echoing stories of past artisans. Visitors can almost hear the soft jingle of bells mingling with laughter as families gather to celebrate the season, binding past to present in a timeless dance of joy. This enchanting atmosphere finds its roots in Germany, inspiring a sense of wonder that turns the chill of winter into the warmest of welcomes.

Nuremberg's Festive Spirit captures all that's magical about Germany's Christmas markets. Nestled in the heart of Bavaria, Nuremberg's Christkindlesmarkt is a quintessential celebration of the season, with its roots reaching back to the 16th century. This market isn't just about shopping; it's a tradition, a way of life, and a heartwarming dive into history and culture that continues to enchant visitors year after year.

As you wander through the cobbled streets, the scents of roasted almonds, spicy gingerbread, and sizzling bratwurst waft through the crisp winter air, tempting every passerby. The aroma alone is enough to conjure images of fairy tale festivities. Stalls are adorned with red and white striped awnings, creating an inviting atmosphere that beckons both locals and travelers to immerse themselves in the holiday spirit.

The Nuremberg Christkindlesmarkt is famed for its opening ceremony, a ritual keenly awaited each year. As evening falls, the spotlight is cast on the prized Nuremberg Christkind — an angelic figure who recites a festive prologue from the balcony of the Frauenkirche. The Christkind, selected every two years, is typically a young woman from Nuremberg who embodies the city's festive spirit, her golden locks and radiant face illuminating the crowd below.

One of the highlights of this market is the craftsmanship displayed at each stall. Vendors, many of whom have been selling their goods here for generations, offer an array of traditional wares. Hand-carved wooden ornaments and intricately painted nutcrackers catch the eye, each item crafted with love and attention to detail. These artisans spend months preparing for this market, ensuring every piece contributes to the authenticity of the experience.

Not to be overshadowed by the artisan goods, the culinary delights of the Christkindlesmarkt are a must-try. Nuremberg is renowned for its Nürnberger Lebkuchen, a distinctive type of gingerbread. This delicacy, spiced with cinnamon, cloves, and nutmeg, often comes topped with a sugar glaze or nuts. Pair this with a steaming mug of glühwein, a traditional mulled wine spiced to perfection, and you have a taste of Christmas that warms the heart as much as it does the soul.

For those traveling with little ones, the Kinderweihnacht offers a magical experience just for them. This children's Christmas market features nostalgic carousels, a miniature Ferris wheel, and even hands-on workshops where children can create their own gifts and ornaments. The sounds of joyful laughter echoing through this part of the market add an extra layer of delight to the entire scene.

Nuremberg's dedication to keeping the Christkindlesmarkt both authentic and environmentally friendly deserves a special mention. In recent years, organizers have shifted towards more sustainable practices — from using LED lights to serving beverages in refundable cups, reducing the market's carbon footprint while still preserving its inherent charm and tradition.

Unsurprisingly, this market doesn't just cater to tourists. Locals frequent the Christkindlesmarkt, sharing fond memories and continuing family traditions that have endured through generations. It's a space where community spirit shines, as people gather to celebrate, shop, and enjoy the simple joys of the season together.

Although it's easy to get lost in the festive hustle and bustle, take a moment to step back and appreciate the historical backdrop of Nuremberg itself. The city, with its medieval architecture and historical sites, adds a layer of depth and character to the Christmas experience. An evening stroll through Nuremberg during the holidays becomes almost a time-traveling venture, offering glimpses into the past amidst the merriment of the present.

As the evening concludes, the glow of twinkling lights dances across Nuremberg's skyline, reflecting the festive joy found in every corner of this enchanting market. It's no wonder visitors often return year after year, drawn back by the promise of new experiences wrapped in the city's ever-present warmth.

Nuremberg's Festive Spirit is not just a section in a travel guide; it's a heartfelt invitation to join a century-old tradition where the past and present mingle amid festive lights, enticing aromas, and the collective cheer of a community brought together by the magic of Christmas.

Dresden's Striezelmarkt Traditions Nestled in the heart of Germany, Dresden's Striezelmarkt is a glorious testament to the enduring magic of European Christmas markets. With over five centuries of history, this celebrated market is not just one of the oldest but also one of the most cherished holiday destinations in the world. Every year, the Altmarkt Square transforms into a vibrant tapestry of traditions, capturing the spirit of Christmas with its enchanting blend of history, crafts, and culinary delights.

The moment you step into the Striezelmarkt, you're enveloped by the inviting aroma of freshly baked stollen, the famous Dresden Christmas cake. The market itself draws its name from the 'Striezel', an early version of this beloved treat. Vendors line their stalls with endless arrays of this fruit-filled bread dusted with powdered sugar, offering slices that are hard to resist. Beyond just a feast for the taste buds, the stollen is a symbol of community and holiday spirit, baked with love and shared with family and friends throughout the season.

Handcrafted treasures are a staple of the Striezelmarkt, where artisans display their skills in creating one-of-a-kind gifts. The Saxon tradition of woodcarving, in particular, shines here with intricate nutcrackers, exquisite pyramids, and delicate candle arches, each piece telling a story of its own. Craftsmanship has been passed down through generations, transforming humble pieces of wood into works of art that bring warmth and magic to any holiday setting. Adding to this, you find booths filled with blown glass ornaments, hand-stitched linens, and fine ceramics, each item a small token of the market's rich heritage.

The centerpiece of the market is the towering Christmas pyramid, which stands proudly over the rows of stalls. This wooden structure, often decorated with tiers of rotating figures and illuminated by candlelight, is a beloved part of Saxon holiday tradition. Its movement and light evoke warmth and merriment, drawing visitors in like moths to a flame. Each year, the pyramid seems to tell a different story, capturing the imagination of all who gather in its glow.

Music, too, plays a pivotal role in Dresden's festive celebrations. The air is alive with the melodies of traditional Christmas carols, performed by local choirs and orchestras. Each note carries with it centuries of tradition and joy, echoing through the market and spreading cheer to even the coldest corners of the square. It's not uncommon to find yourself joining in, swept up by the harmonious blend of voices and instruments that permeate the crisp winter air.

Embrace the warmth of community at Dresden's Striezelmarkt, where the spirit of togetherness is palpable. Locals and tourists alike come together to sip on steaming mugs of Glühwein, a warm mulled wine spiced with cinnamon, cloves, and citrus, perfect for warding off the chill. This simple pleasure is often accompanied by hearty bratwursts and gingerbread, served warm and providing comfort against the wintry air. Conversations flow as easily as the hot drinks, with strangers quick to become friends in the festive environment.

For families, the market is particularly enchanting with its dedicated children's area, where little ones can ride charming carousels and create crafts of their own. The Kinderweihnacht, or Children's Christmas Market, is a wonderland of playful activities, where the magic of the season is brought to life through storytelling, puppet shows, and hands-on workshops. These experiences ensure that the younger generation carries forward the tradition and legacy of the Striezelmarkt.

Visiting the Dresden Striezelmarkt is akin to stepping into a living storybook, where each corner of the market teems with history, tradition, and festive wonder. It's a place where the past meets the present, and where the quintessential charm of a bygone era is preserved and celebrated. Travelers and holiday lovers find themselves captivated by its spell, drawn into a world steeped in heritage and illuminated by the twinkling lights of Christmas.

Dresden's Striezelmarkt isn't just a market; it's an experience. One that invites you to lose yourself in its kaleidoscope of sights, smells, and sounds. Whether it's your first visit or a beloved annual tradition, the market promises memories that are cherished long after the last snowflake has fallen. As you wander through its stalls, you realize that the true magic of the Striezelmarkt lies not just in its physical wares, but in the enduring spirit of community and the joy of connection it inspires.

Austria's Winter Charm

Amidst the snow-draped landscapes and mountainous vistas, Austria's winter charm unfolds like a storybook tale of festivity and warmth. The country's Christmas markets are more than just a feast for the senses; they're a deep dive into the heart of Austrian culture and tradition. Imagine strolling through markets where the air is filled with the enchanting scent of roasted chestnuts and mulled wine, while the stalls brim with artisanal crafts, each reflecting the intricate handiwork that Austrian artisans are renowned for. The twinkle of lights illuminates charming settings that could have sprung from a postcard, inviting travelers to wander and explore. Perspectives shift from awe-inspiring architecture to quaint villages, each promising a unique holiday memory. Whether it's the grand splendor of Vienna's markets or the cozy charm of alpine towns, Austria offers a winter experience that envelops you in its serene beauty, leaving an imprint long after the holiday season has passed.

Vienna's Christmas Dream is like stepping into a winter wonderland, where the air is filled with the sweet scent of roasted chestnuts and the melodic sound of traditional carols. Austria, renowned for its enchanting winter charm, finds its heart in the streets of Vienna during the holiday season. As snow gently blankets the city, Vienna transforms into a realm of festive enchantment, welcoming visitors from around the world to experience its magical Christmas markets.

The city's markets are not just a feast for the eyes; they're a sensory journey where one can indulge in authentic Austrian delights. The Vienna Christmas Dream at Rathausplatz is arguably the most iconic, drawing crowds with its dazzling lights and the comforting aroma of hot mulled wine known as Glühwein. Here, you can feel the city's pulse as locals and visitors mingle amidst stalls adorned with handcrafted gifts, gingerbread, and artisan candles. The towering Christmas tree, a centerpiece, serves as a beacon of joy and celebration.

Wandering through the rows of market stalls, you might stumble upon unique finds—hand-knitted scarves, traditional wooden toys, or beautifully decorated ornaments. These items speak to Austria's rich heritage and craftsmanship, offering glimpses into the artisan culture that thrives in this region. Each piece tells a story, a reflection of Vienna's centuries-old traditions adapted to modern tastes.

Yet, the charm of Vienna's Christmas Dream isn't confined to material souvenirs. It's an experience laced with lasting memories, whether you're savoring a sweet Sachertorte or relishing the warmth of a Fruchtspieß—a delightful chocolate-covered fruit skewer. The Markt can keep you lingering for hours, entranced by street performers singing in harmony with the distant church bells, or the carousel that whirls under a star-studded sky.

Beyond the markets, Vienna's winter charm extends to its cultural offerings. The city pulsates with concerts, plays, and ballet performances, each adding a layer of cultural richness to your visit. The Vienna State Opera and Concert Halls come alive with renditions of classical masterpieces that echo the festive spirit. With historical architecture as a backdrop, experiencing a performance here feels like stepping into a living tapestry of culture and celebration.

Children's laughter fills the air as well, especially around the Ice Dream. This expansive ice rink at the Rathausplatz fulfills every young and old skater's dreams, where they glide hand in hand around twinkling trails. The joy is infectious, and before long, you're swept up in the festive cheer.

Perhaps what's most enchanting about Vienna during this season is how seamlessly the old and new blend together. Baroque architecture adorned with modern light installations creates an ambient glow that invites exploration. The traditional horse-drawn carriages clip-clopping along cobblestoned streets offer a nostalgic thrill, transporting you back in time while you take in the breathtaking cityscapes.

If you're in search of historical allure, the Schönbrunn Palace Christmas Market provides just that. Nestled within the baroque imperial palace grounds, this market is known for its elegance and uniqueness. It's a must-visit spot that perfectly marries the imperial grandeur of Vienna with the cozy charm of a traditional Christmas market. Warm lights set against the majestic palace create an unforgettable sight, evoking feelings of nostalgia and wonder.

Each district, each corner of Vienna seems to embrace the festive spirit, offering a different take on the Christmas market experience. Clark Gable once described Vienna as a city where the spirit of Christmas seemed to live in the very cobblestones. That spirit is tangible today, a testament to Vienna's enduring legacy as a center of art, culture, and celebration.

In conclusion, Vienna's Christmas Dream isn't merely a marketplace; it's a celebration of life and love in the heart of winter. It captures the essence of what makes the holiday season truly magical and invites every visitor to take part in this cultural symphony. As you leave the city with your heart full, you carry with you memories of warmth, joy, and the unmistaken magic that is uniquely Viennese.

Chapter 2:
France's Enchanting Celebrations

In the heart of Europe, France unfurls a tapestry of holiday enchantment that is as diverse as it is captivating. What sets French Christmas markets apart is their blend of tradition and elegance, drawing visitors into a world where history and modernity coalesce with a festive spirit. Imagine wandering through Strasbourg, a city draped in captivating lights that dance off the cobblestones, creating a fairy-tale setting known as the "Capital of Christmas." Each market stall is a beckoning window into local crafts and culinary delights, making it impossible not to indulge in a warm cup of mulled wine. Meanwhile, Paris dazzles with its holiday elegance, where iconic landmarks like the Eiffel Tower become even more enchanting when framed by glittering garlands and twinkling lights reflecting on the Seine. The mixture of sumptuous art, history, and seasonal joy creates a winter wonderland that's uniquely French, offering an inspiring array of experiences set to fill any travel enthusiast with awe and appreciation for the rich festive beauty that France so gracefully presents. Beyond the glittering facades and charming wood-clad stalls, it's the warm embrace of French hospitality and culture that lingers long after the last light dims, inviting you back time and again.

Strasbourg's Captivating Lights

Strasbourg, often coined the "Capital of Christmas," is a veritable wonderland of twinkling lights and festive cheer. Nestled on the border between France and Germany, this enchanting city beautifully blends French elegance with Germanic traditions. It's no wonder that the Strasbourg Christmas Market, known locally as "Christkindelsmärik," holds the title of being the oldest Christmas market in France, dating back to 1570. With its cobblestone streets beautifully adorned with holiday lights and decorations, Strasbourg transforms into a dazzling display that captivates visitors from across the globe.

As the sun dips below the horizon, the city illuminates, casting a soft glow on the half-timbered houses that line the picturesque streets. The magic of Strasbourg's lights begins at the Grande Île, the heart of the city. Here, the Place Kléber hosts a grand Christmas tree, its towering presence adorned with shimmering ornaments and a galaxy of lights—is a sight to behold. This tree, often hailed as the centerpiece of the city's festive celebrations, serves as a symbol of unity and peace during the holiday season.

The twinkling brilliance extends throughout the city, with nearly every street and alley graced with its own set of unique illuminations. The Rue des Grandes Arcades offers an especially breathtaking scene, where intricate displays hang overhead, creating a canopy of lights that guides visitors on a journey through the season's spirit. This pathway not only leads to various market stalls but also to an experience that merges the history and vibrancy of Strasbourg's festive traditions.

Walking through the markets, you're greeted by a sensory feast of holiday aromas—think warm spiced wine, known locally as vin chaud, and the sweet scent of bredele, the traditional Alsatian biscuits found in countless varieties. The flicker of candlelight from stalls illuminates smiling faces as vendors offer handcrafted goods, from delicate ornaments to artisanal toys. Each item tells a story, often of time-honored traditions passed down through generations.

Strasbourg's lighting display doesn't stop in the commercial heart of the city. La Petite France, a historic area characterized by its picturesque medieval buildings, becomes a scene straight out of a fairy tale. The reflection of festive lights on the canals envelops visitors in a 360-degree spectacle. It's easy to lose track of time here, wandering through narrow lanes where every twist and turn reveals a new aspect of the city's illuminated allure.

In addition to the stunning illumination, Strasbourg's festive atmosphere is amplified by various performances and events. Choirs fill the air with joyous carols, echoing through the streets and drawing in passersby. Traditional Alsatian music groups add to the soundscape with lively tunes played on accordions and violins. These melodies, combined with the sights and aromas of the market, create an intoxicating blend that embodies the spirit of Christmas.

The city's dedication to maintaining a tradition of sustainable and responsible festivity is noteworthy. Strasbourg has taken significant steps to ensure its Christmas market and lighting are eco-friendly. Energy-efficient LED lights are used throughout the city, reflecting their commitment to celebrating while also caring for the planet. This environmentally-conscious approach sets a benchmark for other holiday celebrations worldwide.

Throughout the weeks of Advent, special events such as workshops and guided tours delve deeper into Strasbourg's festive heritage. Visitors are invited to partake in candle-making sessions, discover the history behind the city's beloved bredele, and learn about the art of Alsatian crafts. These experiences provide a richer understanding of the cultural significance behind the twinkling lights and joyous celebrations.

In Strasbourg, the light isn't just a visual feast; it represents warmth, welcoming all—locals and travelers alike—to partake in a communal celebration of the holiday spirit. The city's lights serve as a beacon of hospitality, inviting everyone to experience its unique blend of history, culture, and festivity.

The city's allure doesn't end there. For those willing to explore beyond the markets, Strasbourg offers a treasure trove of architectural and cultural marvels, seamlessly woven into the holiday experience. The Strasbourg Cathedral, for instance, presents a soaring spectacle, its iconic façade aglow with careful illumination that highlights its Gothic grandeur. Even at night, the rose window shines as a jewel in the city's crown, offering an awe-striking ascent into history.

Moreover, the illumination of Strasbourg draws visitors into communal spaces. The conviviality at Place de la Cathédrale extends beyond commerce; it's a mosaic of interactions, with locals sharing tales of their traditions and travelers exchanging stories of their journeys. This human connection, fostered under the ambient light, is perhaps the most treasured aspect of Strasbourg's Christmas market.

For those planning their travels to Strasbourg, it's advisable to wander and relish the journey, winding through the illuminated streets at your own pace. Experience the city's light installations both during the twilight that seems to set the city aglow, and at nighttime when the artifices of the day fade, letting the holiday luminescence reign supreme.

Strasbourg's captivating lights don't just illuminate the city; they reveal it in its most festive attire, offering an invitation wrapped in twinkling allure. So consider this an open call to immerse yourself in the warm glow and timeless spirit that the city extends to all who visit. In every corner, under every light, there lies a story—the age-old tale of a city that embraces the Christmas spirit with brilliance, charm, and unyielding hospitality. Unexpected discoveries await beneath the lights of Strasbourg, awaiting those who seek more than just a journey but instead an experience that lingers long after the markets have closed and the lights have dimmed.

Paris's Holiday Elegance

Paris transforms into a city of lights and elegance every holiday season, where the magic of Christmas is woven into every street, showcasing an unmatched festive charm. The City of Light proves that it truly lives up to its name during the holidays, with twinkling lights adorning iconic landmarks and intimate neighborhoods alike. Amidst the ancient cobblestone streets and the sweeping boulevards, Paris offers an enchanting blend of tradition and sophistication that captures the hearts of travelers and locals alike.

Walking down the Champs-Élysées during the holiday season is nothing short of magnificent. This famous avenue, lined with its extravagant boutiques and cafes, becomes a dazzling corridor of light that stretches from the Arc de Triomphe to the Place de la Concorde. The trees along this majestic road are illuminated with thousands of twinkling lights, creating a spectacle that is simply breathtaking. As you stroll along, the sweet aroma of roasted chestnuts fills the air, inviting you to indulge in a quintessentially Parisian, holiday experience.

Beyond the glamour of the Champs-Élysées, the markets of Paris offer an artisan's touch that enchants the soul. The Christmas market at La Défense stands out with its modern backdrop and wide array of regional products, handmade crafts, and gourmet delights. Nestled under the grandeur of skyscrapers, this market offers a unique contrast, blending contemporary vibes with traditional festive cheer. Vendors from various regions of France gather here to showcase their craft, offering everything from hand-knitted scarves to exquisite cheeses.

One cannot mention Parisian elegance without bringing to light Galeries Lafayette's ornate Christmas displays. These legendary department store windows attract visitors annually, each year presenting a different imaginative theme. Under the grand dome inside, a massive Christmas tree rises, adorned in dazzling ornaments, making it a highlight of the Parisian holiday experience. Shopping here during the festive season turns into an event, where every floor of this historic building offers something unique and captivating for its visitors.

In the heart of the city, the Notre-Dame Christmas Market provides a setting rich with history and warmth. While the famed cathedral is a marvel itself, the square surrounding it brims with artisan stands offering intricate crafts and unique souvenirs. This market emphasizes Paris's knack for combining heritage and community spirit, bringing people together amidst holiday songs and warm beverages. It's here, in the shadow of Notre-Dame's gothic splendor, that one might find the perfect handcrafted gift for loved ones.

Parisian holiday elegance transcends shopping and sightseeing, permeating into the culinary delights that celebrate the season. Indulging in a festive meal at a cozy bistro becomes a quintessential part of the experience, where traditional dishes are infused with French finesse. From foie gras and roasted goose to a bûche de Noël beautifully presented, each dish is a masterpiece that reflects France's rich gastronomic heritage. Paired with fine wine, the meals not only warm the stomach but also the spirit, capturing the essence of Parisian hospitality.

Moreover, the city's numerous ice rinks provide seasonal fun that is embraced by both young and old. The rink at the Eiffel Tower, in particular, offers an unforgettable experience. Gliding across the ice with the Iron Lady towering above in the chilly winter air feels almost surreal, a magical moment suspended in time. These ice rinks, scattered throughout the city, create playful spaces where cheerful laughter and the crisp sound of skates cutting through ice echo into the winter air.

To explore Paris's holiday elegance is to engage in a timeless dance of tradition and luxury. Whether it is elegantly lit streets, carefully curated markets, or gourmet culinary experiences, Paris during the holiday season offers something for every taste. Parisians have an innate ability to celebrate with style, making the city not only a visual delight but also a warm embrace of festive cheer. It's a season where past traditions and contemporary celebrations blend seamlessly, inviting one to explore each part of this captivating city.

As you experience Christmas in Paris, the whispers of history, art, and culture are ever-present. The city's museums and galleries often feature special seasonal exhibitions, allowing visitors to dive deeper into Paris's cultural wealth. These exhibitions serve to remind us that Paris is a city where elegance is not confined to the holidays but pervades throughout its vast artistic expressions.

Ultimately, the holiday season in Paris is a time when the city dresses not just in lights but in an atmosphere of inclusion and joy. As carolers sing along the Seine and locals gather for winter strolls in the parks, there is a sense of community and optimism. From glittering lights to the warmth of shared moments, Paris, in its entirety, radiates a unique elegance that enchants every visitor. Here, during the festive season, elegance isn't just an act; it's a way of life, capturing the very essence of the City of Light.

Chapter 3:
The United Kingdom's Festive Delights

In the United Kingdom, Christmas markets transform the bustling cities and quaint towns into enchanting spectacles of holiday cheer. Few places capture the festive spirit like London, where the likes of Hyde Park's Winter Wonderland offer dazzling lights, thrilling rides, and diverse culinary treats beneath sparkling canopies. Moving north, Edinburgh's markets add a distinctly Scottish twist to traditional festivities, nestled beneath the majestic Edinburgh Castle. Here, aromas of mulled wine and roasted chestnuts fill the crisp winter air as bagpipes play in the distance, inviting visitors to immerse themselves in a merry mix of local crafts and international delights. Across the country, from coastal retreats to the heart of the countryside, the UK's Christmas markets offer a unique tapestry of experiences that combine British tradition with global influences, inviting travelers to revel in their festive magic.

London's Winter Wonderland

Imagine stepping into a world where twinkling fairy lights drape every lamppost and tree, where the rich aroma of mulled wine and roasted chestnuts wafts through the air. This is London's Winter Wonderland in Hyde Park, a spectacle that transforms the city's December darkness into an enchanting hub of festive activity. For travel enthusiasts keen to explore the world's finest Christmas markets, this annual event promises a unique blending of tradition and modern amusement, making it an unmissable stop on any festive journey across the United Kingdom.

The grandeur of Winter Wonderland might initially seem overwhelming, but there's a delightful harmony in its chaos. The market is more than a place; it's an experience. Adorned with extensive festive decorations, it hosts an array of attractions ranging from traditional Christmas stalls to thrilling carnival rides. As visitors stroll through the expansive park, they discover a winter village that offers everything from handmade gifts to international cuisines, catering to both the wanderer's heart and the epicure's palate.

What sets London's Winter Wonderland apart is its ability to blend the old with the new. At its heart lies the traditional German-style Christmas market. Rows of wooden chalets brim with unique gifts—crafts, trinkets, and artisanal goods. Here, the stalls echo a charming sense of nostalgia with every handcrafted ornament and beautifully embroidered fabric on display. For those interested in a culinary voyage, the global street food scene offers everything from Bavarian pretzels to gourmet cheese, catering to every taste bud.

An overarching sense of inclusivity marks the ethos of London's Winter Wonderland. This spirit is perhaps best embodied in its diverse entertainment offerings. The real jewel for many is the ice-skating rink, London's largest, nestled amongst the festive glow of Victorian lamps. For families, there's the Magical Ice Kingdom, an impressively sculpted icy world that enthralls with its glittering fantasies and mystical creatures. Meanwhile, live performances, including circus acts and musical shows, add another layer of vivacity, ensuring that there's something for everyone to marvel at.

Still, for all its delights, it is the atmosphere of Winter Wonderland that remains its most enchanting element. Step onto the grounds, and you're immediately enveloped by an ambient orchestra of Christmas carols harmonizing with the rhythmic calls of amusement attractions.

Children's laughter mingles with the gentle clinking of glasses, where visitors toast to the festive cheer. This joyous soundscape, amplified by the palpable sense of excitement, makes Hyde Park, during this time, nothing short of magical.

London's Winter Wonderland is, without doubt, a testament to the city's love for celebrations. It's a vivid reminder that, while modern London is a bustling metropolis, its heart still beats to the rhythm of tradition, community, and festivity. Each year, it reimagines the very essence of Christmas joy, offering not just a market, but a microcosm of global holiday spirit, right in the heart of the British capital.

With every turn, London's Winter Wonderland invites us to explore its multitude of experiences, beckoning both the unsuspecting passerby and the seasoned traveler. It's a celebration of the little things—a warm cup of cocoa shared with a friend amidst falling snow, the discovery of a perfect handmade ornament, or merely the simple act of gazing at the shimmering winter sky, reminding us of the joy in these fleeting moments of wonder.

Edinburgh's Magical Markets

Nestled amidst the picturesque hills of Scotland, Edinburgh transforms into a wonderland of festive cheer during the holiday season. Every winter, as the nights grow longer, the city dons its enchanting cloak of Christmas magic, inviting travelers and locals alike to explore its historic streets lined with stalls brimming with seasonal delights. The air is filled with the rich aromas of mulled wine and roasted chestnuts, drawing visitors in with promises of warmth and indulgence. Edinburgh's Christmas markets, a fusion of tradition and innovation, are an essential stop for anyone seeking a quintessentially British holiday experience.

Central to Edinburgh's festive celebrations is the European Market, a vibrant spectacle set against the stunning backdrop of the city's cultural heart, Princes Street Gardens. With the majestic Edinburgh Castle looming elegantly above, the market sprawls across both sides of the street. Upon entering, visitors are greeted by a dazzling array of lights, guiding them through a labyrinth of wooden chalets adorned with handcrafted goods and artisan food offerings. It's a feast for the senses, with intricate glass ornaments glinting in the winter sun and the tantalizing scent of Scottish shortbread inviting you to take a closer look.

One of the unique aspects of Edinburgh's markets is their ability to blend Scottish heritage with international flair. Amongst the stalls, you'll discover craftspeople showcasing traditional Scottish wares; think luxurious cashmere scarves, rugged Harris Tweed jackets, and heirloom-quality tartan blankets. These are interspersed with stalls selling global treasures, from German bratwurst and Belgian chocolates to French crepes, capturing the cosmopolitan spirit of the event. This harmonious blend attracts an eclectic mix of visitors, fostering a sense of unity and shared joy that resonates throughout the city.

Over in St Andrew Square, the East Princes Street Gardens hosts the Scottish Market, where the focus shifts more towards local craftsmanship and culinary delights. It's here that the strength of Scottish enterprise truly shines, offering visitors an authentic taste of the region's traditions. Artisans proudly display their jams made from local berries, single malt whiskies aged to perfection, and artisanal cheeses that reflect the rich agricultural heritage of the Scottish Highlands. Among the favorites are the savory haggis bonbons and the ever-popular Celtic Cuisine hog roast, which consistently draw long lines of eager food lovers.

But Edinburgh's markets offer more than just shopping and eating; they provide a full sensory experience that transforms a simple stroll into a journey of discovery. Musicians playing jigs and reels add a lively soundtrack as you wander. The sound of bagpipes intertwines with holiday tunes, setting a joyful rhythm to your steps. Street performers spot the markets, engaging audiences with magic tricks and interactive plays that delight children and adults alike. This lively atmosphere is infectious, spreading holiday cheer throughout the crowd.

For families, a visit to Edinburgh's markets is often not complete without a stop at Santa Land in West Princes Street Gardens. This whimsical realm is designed with children in mind, featuring a variety of rides and attractions, from the classic carousel to the thrilling Santa Train Ride. Here, kids can meet Santa Claus in person, presenting the perfect opportunity to capture those unforgettable holiday memories. The enchanting Christmas Tree Maze challenges young adventurers to navigate its twists and turns, while a nearby ice cave offers a magical grotto experience.

A jewel of the Scottish capital, the Festival Square Spiegeltent, showcases another dimension of holiday charm with its lineup of Christmas shows and performances. This vintage traveling venue, reminiscent of the 19th-century wooden tent structures of Europe, is replete with mirrors and stained glass, offering a cozy yet grand setting for an array of entertainment. From Christmas-themed plays and lively music concerts to dance performances, there's something here to captivate every audience.

Edinburgh's markets come alive in the evening, bathed in the glow of innumerable lights. The city landscape changes as buildings, monuments, and even the towering Ferris wheel are illuminated, casting reflections across the streets and parks. A ride on this vintage-style observation wheel grants you a breathtaking view of the twinkling cityscape, with the Firth of Forth visible on the horizon. Such moments of serene beauty encapsulate the spirit of Edinburgh's festive season and leave an indelible mark on visitors' memories.

The markets serve not only as a hub of festive activity but also as a stage for cultural exchange and community engagement. Pop-up activities and workshops bring people together to learn and share, whether it's crafting Christmas wreaths from foraged materials or brewing a traditional Scottish ale. Visitors can watch demonstrations from skilled craftsmen or even try their hand at a new skill, from pottery making to culinary arts, offering insights into Edinburgh's rich cultural tapestry.

As one ventures through the city's holiday offerings, it's clear that Edinburgh's markets are a celebration of diversity, creativity, and joy. The vibrant atmosphere, welcoming spirit, and captivating setting make them a must-see on any festive itinerary. These markets offer an exemplar of the holiday magic that envelops the United Kingdom, tempting anyone with a taste for tradition and a love of exploration to embrace the beauty and warmth they promise. Whether it's your first visit or a cherished annual event, Edinburgh's magical markets provide endless inspiration and a heartfelt reminder of the simple pleasures of the festive season.

Chapter 4:
The Nordic Yuletide Experience

Stepping into the Nordic Yuletide Experience is like entering a winter wonderland where tradition meets mystique, promising an enchanting blend of snowy landscapes and age-old customs. Picture Sweden's starry nights, where the air is crisp and the red-and-white stalls overflow with handcrafted gifts that tell stories of Swedish folklore. Meanwhile, Finland offers a magical embrace, with snow-draped forests and the undeniable allure of Santa Claus's homeland, where every snowflake seems to sparkle a little brighter. It's a season where the cozy glow of candle-lit windows and the laughter from outdoor markets fill the soul with warmth against the frosty Nordic chill. Whether you're sipping on steaming glögg or watching intricate ice sculptures come to life, these winter celebrations invite travelers to immerse themselves in a unique tapestry of cultural richness and festive joy that only the Nordics can offer. It's a place where the holiday spirit is as bold and invigorating as the winter air itself.

Sweden's Seasonal Splendor

As the days grow shorter and the temperatures drop, Sweden transforms into a wonderland of winter enchantment, draped in lights and filled with the spirit of Christmas. The Nordic winter, with its long nights, is not something to be endured here but rather celebrated with fervor, warmth, and tradition. Sweden's unique way of marking the Yuletide is not merely a season but a deep-rooted cultural tapestry woven with threads of history, folklore, and community spirit.

Sweden's commitment to holiday celebration is evident in the vibrant Christmas markets that spring up across its cities and countryside. In Stockholm, the Old Town's Stortorget Christmas market is a vivid spectacle, generously adorned with thousands of twinkling lights, and it boasts an enviable reputation for offering traditional Swedish handicrafts and Christmas delicacies. A walk through the market is like stepping into a bygone era where the past and present collide in harmonious celebration. The scent of glögg—a spiced, warm mulled wine—mingles with the inviting aroma of traditional Swedish pastries like saffransbullar, tempting locals and visitors alike.

While Stockholm holds the heart of Sweden's seasonal celebration, it's the smaller towns where the magic truly feels personal and quaint. The city of Gothenburg turns into the 'Christmas City', captivating its visitors with Liseberg amusement park's winter transformation. Here, the market nods to wintry dreams and childhood nostalgia with its lovingly decorated stalls and an open-air ice-skating rink, inviting anyone to glide under the starlit sky. It's a place where laughter and joy are as warm as the mugs of hot chocolate cradled by gloved hands.

Travel north to the ice-laden expanses of Lapland and you'll discover a different side of Sweden's festive offerings. Besides being world-renowned for its natural beauty, Lapland offers a unique chance to meet Santa Claus in his Arctic habitat at the Santa Claus Village. Here, the magic of the season gains a celestial quality under the dance of the Northern Lights, a spectacle worth every shiver and every mile travelled to reach this enchanting corner of the world.

Part of what makes Sweden's holiday season so enriching is its deep connection to age-old traditions that are still very much alive. Luciadagen, or Saint Lucia's Day, is one such celebration that gives the dark winter days a new light. Celebrated on December 13th, this festival is characterized by candlelit processions led by girls dressed in white robes with crowns of candles on their heads. It's a stunning visual and cultural counterpoint to the commercial festivities, demonstrating Sweden's reverence for light during the darkest time of the year.

Another remarkable feature of the Swedish festive season is the diversity in the markets themselves. Malmö, for instance, embraces a more cosmopolitan approach, integrating influences from around the globe into its holiday celebrations, which reflect the city's multicultural population. Visitors are equally likely to encounter stalls offering marzipan and gingerbread as they are to find exotic spices and handmade ornaments from artisans who have made Malmö their home.

The Swedish countryside plays host to some of the coziest Christmas experiences that travelers can wish for. Traditional red cottages, covered with layers of snow, welcome guests to taste home-cooked meals that highlight locally-sourced ingredients. Imagine tasting freshly baked pepparkakor, a type of ginger snap, while watching the serene snowfall sparkle under dimming daylight. Panning around these small villages, the sense of community and collective celebration is palpable.

For those looking for a deeper dive into Sweden's winter wonders, the town of Jukkasjärvi offers one of the most novel accommodations: the Icehotel. Every year, this hotel is painstakingly sculpted anew from ice harvested from the Torne River. Staying here becomes more than an overnight adventure—it's an unforgettable experience to complement the market tour. With its elaborately carved rooms and halls, the Icehotel is as much an art gallery as it is a place to sleep.

As the holiday season unfolds, it's clear that each region of Sweden offers something distinctive—whether it be through unique crafts, culinary delights, or local Yuletide celebrations. But what unites them all is a consistent warmth and hospitality. These are not just seasonal markets—they are gatherings that embrace all who come with open arms, inviting them to experience not just the holiday spirit but the essence of Swedish culture itself.

Sweden's Christmas markets are not just about shopping and indulgence; they're about finding something genuine, something perhaps long-forgotten but always recalled—joy, simplicity, community. This is a place where the natural beauty of the season meets the handcrafted artistry of its people, creating a scene that's both timeless and magical. As the soft snowflakes fall against a backdrop of century-old traditions and flickering candles, Sweden offers an irresistible glimpse of the season's true splendor.

Finland's Snowy Celebrations

Imagine stepping into a world where the crisp air tingles with the promise of snow, and the horizon is a canvas painted with hues of white and evergreen. Welcome to Finland's snowy celebrations, a place where the magic of Christmas is felt in every drifting snowflake and echoed in the tranquility of its frost-covered landscapes. In Finland, the Yuletide experience is deeply rooted in nature's beauty and age-old traditions that weave stories of warmth and wonder.

The Finnish capital, Helsinki, transforms into a winter wonderland, offering a myriad of festive experiences. The city center bustles with twinkling lights and bustling Christmas markets that embody the Nordic festive spirit. The St. Thomas Christmas Market at the Senate Square is a highlight, with its charming wooden stalls brimming with local crafts, artisanal goods, and heart-warming holiday treats. The scent of smoky glögi—a spiced mulled wine unique to

Finland—wafts through the air, inviting visitors to take a moment to pause and enjoy the warmth amidst the chill.

The markets aren't just about shopping; they provide an immersive glimpse into Finnish culture. Traditionally dressed vendors offer culinary delights that tell stories of the land's rich history. Savory pastries like karjalanpiirakka, a rye pastry filled with creamy rice porridge, and the sweet, cardamom-infused pulla bread serve as delicious anchors for conversations, connecting people to centuries-old Finnish culinary traditions. The sound of cheerful carolers, harmonizing voices singing both in Finnish and Swedish, the country's other official language, adds to the enchanting atmosphere.

As the sun sets early and the night draws in, Helsinki's Christmas lights compete with the natural aurora borealis further north, casting a gentle glow over the festivities. The illumination ceremony, an annual event, serves as the official start to the holiday season, drawing locals and tourists alike. Streets and buildings adorned with intricate light displays exemplify Nordic craftsmanship and capture the simplicity and elegance that Finnish design is celebrated for worldwide.

For those willing to venture beyond the capital, Lapland offers an even more magical Christmas experience. Nestled deep in the Arctic Circle, Lapland is synonymous with Christmas. Rovaniemi, considered the official hometown of Santa Claus, is a must-visit. Here, the Santa Claus Village captivates visitors of all ages. Nestled amid snowy forests, it offers a year-round holiday atmosphere, complete with the opportunity to meet Santa himself. Imagine the joy of crossing the Arctic Circle's latitudinal line, knowing you've reached a place where dreams and reality seamlessly coexist.

Every Finnish town celebrates with its unique blend of tradition and innovation. In Turku, the country's former capital, the Christmas Peace Declaration is a revered tradition dating back to the 13th century. Each year on Christmas Eve, the town gathers to listen to the solemn declaration read aloud from the balcony of the Brinkkala House, urging all to embrace the spirit of goodwill and harmony.

If adventure beckons, then consider partaking in uniquely Finnish outdoor activities. In Finland, winter sports become a key part of the holiday experience. Dog sledding, snowshoeing, and cross-country skiing offer adventures against the backdrop of endless snowy panoramas. One might also partake in a traditional sauna experience, an integral part of Finnish culture. Follow it up with a brisk roll in the snow or a dip in a frozen lake, if you're brave! There's something invigorating about these rituals that captures the heart and warms the soul.

During the long winter nights, the northern skies often grace observers with mesmerizing auroras. Few experiences rival the magic of witnessing this celestial phenomenon, known locally as revontulet, from a cozy log cabin or a swanky glass igloo in the northern regions. It's a spectacle that reinforces Finland's mystical allure, a dance of lights across the heavens that embodies the wonder and serenity of the Nordic winter.

Amidst the celebrations, Finland's penchant for sustainability and simplicity shines through. Christmas trees are often harvested sustainably from nearby forests, and holiday decorations prioritize natural and recycled materials, reflecting Finland's commitment to environmental consciousness. This aspect of minimalism not only enhances the aesthetic but also preserves the essence of Finnish traditions—comfortable, unpretentious, and deeply connected to nature.

Indeed, Finland's snowy celebrations offer a gateway into a world where time seems to slow down, and the hustle and bustle of modern life are temporarily forgotten. It's an invitation to experience a Christmas that feels both ancient and timeless, one that draws from the deep well of Finnish folklore and community spirit. There's a sense of wonderment here, where simplicity finds its stride amidst the snow-laden branches and twinkling lights. Whether sipping warm glögi by a fire, engaging in spirited conversations at a market, or marveling at the ethereal northern lights, Finland offers a Christmas experience that speaks to both the heart and the imagination.

Chapter 5: Spain's Holiday Fervor

Spain bursts with holiday fervor in December, transforming its cities into warm, vibrant canvases of festive cheer. The blend of tradition and modernity creates an atmosphere that's both nostalgic and exhilarating. Streets glow with lights and holiday music fills the air as vendors line the plazas, offering everything from handcrafted gifts to tantalizing treats. Madrid and Barcelona, the giants of Spanish culture, each bring their unique vibes to the holiday table. In Madrid, storied markets allure with intricate nativity scenes and the sweet aroma of churros wafting through the crisp winter air. Barcelona, on the other hand, enchants with its innovative displays and merry parades weaving through Gaudi's architectural masterpieces. One can't help but be swept away by the sheer diversity and spirit of celebration that permeates every corner, inviting visitors to slow down and savor this quintessentially Spanish holiday experience.

Barcelona's Festive Flair

Nestled along the northeastern coast of the Iberian Peninsula, Barcelona is a city that melds its Catalan heart with the vibrant spirit of Christmas. As the holiday season approaches, the city transforms into a tapestry of lights, sounds, and aromas that captivate locals and visitors alike. The streets are decked out in festive decor, from twinkling fairy lights to ornately decorated Christmas trees, leaving no corner untouched by festive charm. Barcelona embraces the holiday fervor with both traditional customs and modern flair, uniting old-world charm with contemporary creativity.

Wandering through Barcelona during Christmas feels like entering a lively painting where every stroke adds warmth and color. The city's historic neighborhoods, like the Gothic Quarter, capture the imagination with their narrow streets illuminated by warm light and the sound of carolers echoing under ancient arches. It's impossible not to feel the infectious energy that permeates this part of the city, as its labyrinthine streets invite exploration of cozy cafes and unique boutiques, each bursting with holiday specials and local delights.

At the heart of Barcelona's Christmas festivities lies Fira de Santa Llúcia, the city's oldest and most renowned Christmas market. This market has been a staple of holiday celebrations since 1786, offering a vast array of handcrafted goods and traditional Catalan decorations. The buzzing stalls feature everything from intricate nativity scenes to colorful poinsettias and quirky Caga Tió, the whimsical wooden log that is lovingly cared for in Catalan homes only to miraculously "poop" presents on Christmas Eve. Browsing through the market stalls, it's easy to get lost in stories behind every handcrafted item, each reflecting the artisans' dedication and cultural pride.

Food, as in many parts of Spain, is a pivotal part of the holiday celebrations. In Barcelona, the festive season dishes are nothing short of culinary poetry. Restaurants and homes alike serve up hearty helpings of escudella i carn d'olla, a traditional Christmas stew bursting with meats and vegetables. The rich aroma of churros, dusted with sugar and served with thick, velvety chocolate, fills the air, a treat which locals and tourists eagerly indulge in while strolling around the city. Local bakeries tempt passersby with turrón, a nougat confection that combines almonds and honey to create a sweet, addictive delight that few can resist.

A particularly captivating tradition in Barcelona is the celebration of the Feast of the Three Kings, or "La Cabalgata de los Reyes Magos," held on the 5th of January. This procession marks the arrival of the Three Wise Men with festivities that include vibrant parades replete with elaborate floats, music, and dancing. Children line the streets, eagerly awaiting the candy tossed from the passing floats, their eyes wide with excitement. For many, this celebration is as momentous as Christmas itself, bringing families together to share in the joy and anticipation of this special occasion.

Beyond markets and parades, Barcelona offers a wealth of experiences that capture the spirit of the holidays. A walk along Passeig de Gràcia becomes a visual delight with the avenue's designer storefronts, all adorned with luxury holiday displays that sparkle under the night sky. Gaudí's architectural masterpieces, such as Casa Batlló and La Pedrera, are illuminated in festive illumination, drawing crowds to witness these iconic landmarks in all their seasonal splendor.

Yet, Barcelona's festive flair isn't solely about the visuals. Music plays a pivotal role in the city's holiday celebration. From traditional Catalan carols to more contemporary performances, concerts and events fill the city's calendar. Venues like the Gran Teatre del Liceu and the Palau de la Música Catalana host enchanting performances that range from classical ballets to choral concerts, each leaving audiences spellbound with their melodic renditions of holiday favorites.

For those seeking solitude amidst the holiday hustle, a visit to the beach provides a serene escape. It may seem unconventional to think of the beach during winter, but Barcelona's mild Mediterranean climate makes it possible to enjoy a seashell-strewn shoreline. The gentle lapping of waves provides a peaceful backdrop for reflection and appreciation of the holiday season, a momentary pause from the energetic festivities of the urban setting just steps away.

As night falls, Barcelona truly comes alive. Holiday lights cast a magical glow over the city, inviting visitors to experience its vibrant nightlife. Tapas bars serve festive selections that pair traditional flavors with innovative twists, accompanied by fine catalan wines or the region's signature cava, a sparkling wine that adds a celebratory fizz to any gathering. For night owls, the city's clubs and salsa bars offer a unique fusion of holiday cheer and Barcelona's legendary entertainment, a cultural convergence that ensures unforgettable memories.

Barcelona's festive allure isn't limited to visual and social experiences alone. The city radiates an inclusive spirit that invites everyone into its yuletide embrace. Residents and tourists alike are drawn to its welcoming atmosphere, where the joy of the season transcends linguistic and cultural boundaries, fostering unity and goodwill.

In Barcelona, Christmas is not merely a holiday; it's an experience that dances across all senses. It's a place where the past and present entwine in a merry embrace, allowing its visitors to step into a living storybook replete with the sights, sounds, and flavors of a city that knows how to celebrate with flair. The memories you make in this city not only last a season but provide stories and moments to cherish for a lifetime.

Madrid's Merry Traditions

To step into Madrid during the festive season is to enter a world where tradition and modernity dance together under the city's twinkling lights. Known for its lively energy and passion, Madrid doesn't shy away from putting on a spectacular Christmas show. The streets sparkle with decorations, and every plaza hums with the sound of holiday music. It's as if the entire city has been wrapped in a cozy, festive blanket.

One of the focal points of Madrid's Christmas celebrations is the Plaza Mayor, a square that dates back to the 17th century. Here, the traditional Christmas market unfolds with stalls that overflow with holiday fare. Vendors offer everything from Iberian ham to churros dipped in thick, rich chocolate. The air is filled with a medley of sweet, enticing aromas that invite visitors to indulge in the unique flavors of a Spanish Christmas. There's a certain warmth to the bustling market, with families wrapped up against the winter chill, sharing laughter and stories.

Beyond the hustle and bustle of shopping, the heart of Madrid's merry traditions lies in its enduring customs. One beloved tradition is the Nativity scene or "Belén." Spaniards take great pride in crafting these intricate displays, often depicting a miniature village alongside the Biblical scene. In Madrid, you can find monumental Nativity scenes set up in churches, public spaces, and even private homes open to the public. The Royal Palace's scene is particularly breathtaking, spanning several rooms and captivating visitors with its attention to detail.

Madrid's festive fervor also finds expression in its vibrant parades. The Three Kings' Parade, or "Cabalgata de Reyes," is a highlight of the holiday season. On the evening of January 5th, exuberantly decorated floats proceed through the streets, reenacting the arrival of the Three Wise Men. For both children and adults, this spectacle is a magical moment, as candy rains down from the passing floats and wide-eyed children wave to their favorite characters.

While much of Madrid's celebration is steeped in tradition, the city also embraces modern elements, making for a unique blend of old and new. Hefty light displays enliven avenues like Gran Vía and Calle de Alcalá. These modern illuminations are the handiwork of renowned designers and bring a contemporary edge to the city's festive appearance. Alongside the traditional Nativity and market stalls, these lights encapsulate how Madrid honors its past while celebrating its present.

For those wanting a break from the cold, Madrid's cultural institutions offer a reprieve with a seasonal twist. The Prado Museum, Reina Sofía, and Thyssen-Bornemisza host Christmas-themed exhibitions and events that appeal to art lovers and curious tourists alike. These experiences provide both insight and warmth, cultivating a deeper connection to Spain's rich cultural tapestry.

Food, naturally, is a central part of Madrid's seasonal experience, and holiday dining offers a tantalizing exploration of Spanish cuisine. Restaurants and cafes roll out special Christmas menus featuring festive specialties like "turrón," a nougat dessert, and "marzipan," both of which are essential during this festive period. For those with a penchant for tradition, the holiday dish "Sopa de Almendra," a delicate almond soup, is a must-try. Family gatherings around these meals highlight the community spirit that defines Madrid's Christmas atmosphere.

Madrid also extends its charm through a rich tapestry of music and dance during holilday concerts and flamenco performances that abound throughout the city. These events are not just spectacles but celebrations of life and joy, ensuring everyone has the chance to partake in Madrid's festive mood. Tailored performances, often held in historic venues, add a layer of elegance and cultural depth to the holiday experience.

The Madrileños—inhabitants of Madrid—have a unique zest for life that shines brightly during the festive season. This exuberance is reflected in all aspects of the Christmas celebrations, making visitors feel like part of a large, joyful family. The city's ability to blend joyous celebration and deep-rooted tradition creates an atmosphere where memories are made and cherished for years to come.

For a travel enthusiast or holiday lover, experiencing Madrid's Christmas is akin to opening a carefully wrapped gift brimming with surprises. From intimate family traditions to public celebrations, each element adds to the city's festive allure. Madrid, with its merry traditions, offers a holiday celebration that is not only exhilarating but deeply enriching. As each corner of the city unfolds its unique charm, it warmly invites you to join in the revelry, leaving you inspired by the festive beauty and cultural richness that define a Madrid Christmas.

Chapter 6:
Italy's Christmas Artistry

As we move from Spain's vibrant traditions, Italy invites us into a captivating world where Christmas is an art form, meticulously crafted from generations of passion and devotion. From the grand operatic displays to humble nativity scenes, Italy blends its renowned artistic legacy with the warmth of the festive season. In Florence, the air buzzes with creativity as artisans turn markets into open-air galleries, offering hand-painted ceramics and intricate jewelry that tell Italy's rich stories. Journey to Rome, and you'll find a fusion of the sacred and celebratory, where Vatican City's timeless elegance presides over bustling piazzas adorned with dazzling lights and aromatic delicacies like panettone and torrone. Italy's Christmas artistry is a vivid tapestry of history, tradition, and heartfelt expression, drawing the festive enthusiast into a realm where every corner holds a masterpiece waiting to be discovered.

Florence's Artisanal Wonders

Nestled in the heart of Tuscany, Florence transforms into a wondrous landscape of artistry and tradition come Christmastime. As the brisk winter air settles and the city is draped in festive decor, local artisans take center stage, showcasing their centuries-old crafts that tell stories of passion, history, and skill.

The essence of Florence's Christmas markets lies in their connection to meticulous craftsmanship. From intricate jewelry pieces molded by expert hands to hand-painted ceramics that capture the rustic charm of the countryside, the markets are a celebration of individuality and heritage. Each vendor not only offers a product but shares a piece of Florentine soul, creating an intimate and personal shopping experience.

Wandering through the bustling squares, one can't help but be charmed by the assortment of handmade leather goods. Florence is renowned for its leatherwork, and during the festive season, stalls brim with expertly crafted bags, wallets, belts, and more, each showcasing the soft texture and unmistakable aroma of high-quality leather. These artisans, often from families that have practiced the craft for generations, infuse each item with a unique character and resilience.

Amidst the festive atmosphere, another sensory delight awaits: the art of traditional textiles. As you stroll past the vibrant market displays, the woven patterns and dazzling colors of hand-loomed scarves and throws catch the eye. These textiles are emblematic of Florence's rich Renaissance history, where textile production played a pivotal role in the city's economic prowess. Purchasing such a piece not only supports the local economy but ensures the continuation of a storied craft.

Florence's Christmas markets are also a treasure trove for food enthusiasts. The culinary offerings present an array of opportunities to savor the flavors of Tuscany. From wells of rich, golden olive oil to baskets of sun-dried tomatoes and jars of balsamic vinegar, each product brings the taste of the Italian sun to the holiday table. The stalls carrying artisanal cheeses and fresh truffles are a gourmand's paradise, inviting taste buds on a delightful journey through the Tuscan hills.

No visit to these markets would be complete without indulging in the region's sweetest delights. Here, the prevalence of Panforte—a dense, nutty cake flavored with spices and fruit—encapsulates a slice of

Italian festive tradition. Each bite tells a tale, transporting one back to an era where such confections were a symbol of luxury and holiday spirit.

Amid these artisanal wonders, there's room for creative expression beyond the traditional. The city's vibrant artisan community continuously innovates, blending ancient techniques with modern aesthetics. You'll find experimental crafts that use sustainable materials, offering eco-conscious travelers a chance to purchase meaningful gifts with minimal environmental impact.

Beyond the material offerings, Florence's markets provide a plentitude of intangible wonders. The atmosphere is one of warmth and hospitality, as vendors eagerly share the history behind their works. It's here where the authentic connection between maker and customer thrives, leaving visitors with more than just a purchase—a cherished experience that embodies the spirit of the season and the heart of Florentine culture.

As night falls and the city's elaborate decorations flicker to life, the essence of Florence at Christmas becomes a canvas of glowing lights and jubilant laughter. Musicians serenade with classic carols, their notes echoing through the cobblestone paths, inviting an impromptu dance under twinkling stars. This is where the true magic of the season is found—in shared moments of joy and artistry.

Venturing through Florence's Christmas markets, it's impossible not to admire the harmony of history and innovation represented in each stall. The markets are a testament to the city's commitment to honoring its artistic roots while embracing the future with creativity and optimism. Each year, they remind us of the timeless allure of hand-crafted wonders and the unyielding spirit of artisans who keep these traditions alive.

For travelers, Florence offers not just a chance to explore Italy's Christmas artistry but also a deeper understanding of the human spirit's capacity to create beauty even in the simplest of things. This celebration is a wellspring of inspiration, inviting all who wander through Florence's vibrant streets to become part of its enduring legacy of artistry and wonder.

Florence's artisanal wonders have long enchanted visitors, and during Christmas, this enchantment is magnified, resonating with the festive warmth that embraces the city. It's a reminder of the beauty that human hands can create, a poetic testament to the joyous spirit of the season, and an invitation for all to take part in its enduring magic.

Rome's Religious and Festive Blend

In the heart of Italy, Rome stands as a testament to both its grand religious past and vibrant festive present, and during the Christmas season, the Eternal City truly comes alive. The air grows crisp and filled with the aroma of roasted chestnuts and freshly baked biscotti. The streets, lined with twinkling lights and decorated trees, lead both locals and visitors to a celebration that marries the sacred with the joyous in a uniquely Roman way.

Rome's deep-rooted Catholic heritage takes center stage during Christmas, transforming the city into a spiritual haven. Pilgrims from all over the world flock to the Vatican to witness the Midnight Mass at St. Peter's Basilica. Under Michelangelo's dome, the experience is nothing short of ethereal, as the Pope delivers a sermon broadcast around the globe. Whether devoutly religious or simply drawn to the historical significance, the shared experience of this solemn event transcends cultural and religious boundaries.

Yet, amidst this religious gravity, there's a lighter, more festive side of Christmas in Rome that simply cannot be overlooked. Piazza Navona, known year-round for its stunning Baroque architecture, hosts one of the city's most famed Christmas markets. Stall after stall, vendors offer nativity scenes, handcrafted ornaments, and traditional Italian sweets. The ambiance is cheerful, inviting everyone to linger a bit longer, to sip on a cup of cioccolata calda while listening to the street performers sing familiar carols.

Nativity scenes, or "presepi" as they are known in Italian, are perhaps the most iconic symbols of Christmas in Rome. Throughout the city, you'll find immensely detailed and artistic displays, ranging from miniature tableaus in churches to life-sized recreations in public squares. Each presepe tells its own story, featuring local figures from everyday Roman life—pizzaiolos, market vendors, and even figures representing famous Roman artists from history. These scenes encapsulate Rome's unique ability to blend the sacred with the everyday, honoring both the birth of Christ and the essence of Roman culture.

The festive season in Rome is also a sensory delight. Enchant your taste buds with traditional Roman holiday treats like panettone and pandoro, rich with raisins and candied fruits. Many Roman families gather together to make struffoli, little fried dough balls coated in honey and sprinkles, or the even more indulgent torrone—a nougat confection that varies in ingredients and flavors, from almond to chocolate. Whether indulging in a sweet pastry from a local pasticceria or immersing yourself in family kitchen traditions, the flavors of Rome at Christmas are unforgettable.

Exploring Rome during this time also means experiencing its myriad holiday events and spectacles. The annual Christmas concert in the beautiful Auditorium Parco della Musica is unmissable, showcasing world-class performers in a setting that marries stunning architecture with sublime acoustics. In another part of the city, opera houses offer seasonal programs, giving visitors the chance to experience the world-renowned Italian operatic tradition in all its glory.

Beyond the markets, nativity scenes, and culinary wonders, the simple act of wandering the historic streets of Rome during Christmastime can be profoundly moving. The city's famed sites—the Colosseum, the Pantheon, the Roman Forum—take on a gentle glow under the festive lights, their ancient stones whispering stories of Christmases past. It's a time when the ancient and the contemporary meld seamlessly, offering both a celebration of history and the joy of presence.

Rome's festive spirit is not merely confined to the limits of tradition; it's dynamic, much like the city itself. As families gather for the seasonal highlight, La Befana on January 6th, the Epiphany Feast, the ancient Piazza della Rotonda once again fills with laughter and merriment. Children anticipate the arrival of Befana, the friendly witch bearing gifts, a figure rich in folklore yet embraced in modern festivities with enthusiasm. This tradition epitomizes the unique Italian ability to weave historical legend with modern celebration seamlessly.

Every corner of Rome seems to offer something magical during Christmas. Walk amongst the softly illuminated ruins at the foot of the Capitoline Hill, or find solace in the quiet moments inside a small chapel off a winding alley. Christmas in Rome is as much about grand spectacles as it is about intimate moments of reflection and joy, each contributing to an experience steeped in both reverence and revelry.

In essence, Rome's Christmas artistry encapsulates a grand tapestry of experiences that are as varied as they are enchanting. It is a season that welcomes everyone into its fold, encouraging all to savor its multifaceted celebrations. So, whether you come for the spiritual solace or the festive cheer—or, more likely, a bit of both—Rome welcomes you with open arms. This ancient city invites you to partake in its enduring blend of reverence and joy, creating memories that linger long after the last Christmas lights fade away.

Chapter 7:
Switzerland's Alpine Markets

Perched majestically amid the snow-capped peaks, Switzerland's Alpine markets offer a uniquely enchanting holiday experience that captivates every travel enthusiast with their breathtaking scenery and festive cheer. Zurich, with its bustling city squares, transforms into a winter wonderland where the aroma of mulled wine and roasted chestnuts fills the air, inviting visitors to explore wooden stalls brimming with handcrafted treasures and seasonal delicacies. Meanwhile, Lucerne's lakeside charm offers a picturesque setting that sparkles with twinkling lights reflected on serene waters, creating a magical ambiance perfect for festive exploration. These markets not only highlight the allure of Swiss craftsmanship but also foster a warm sense of community, as locals and travelers alike gather to celebrate the traditions of the season in an atmosphere of joyous camaraderie. This chapter inspires you to embrace the harmonious blend of tradition and splendor found in Switzerland's Alpine markets, promising a holiday experience unlike any other.

Zurich's Christmas Markets

The magic of Zurich's Christmas markets is where tradition intertwines with modernity, presenting a festive experience that's genuinely enchanting. Zurich, known for its banking and financial prowess, transforms into a winter wonderland as the Christmas season approaches. Imagine walking through the city's historic Old Town, where the scent of mulled wine, roasted chestnuts, and gingerbread fills the air. The streets look like they're from a storybook, adorned with twinkling lights and festive decorations that draw both locals and tourists into a celebration of yuletide joy.

One of the most iconic places to experience this winter transformation is the Zurich Hauptbahnhof, the city's bustling train station, which hosts the Christkindlimarkt. As one of the largest indoor Christmas markets in Europe, this market is a marvel in itself. It's not just the size that impresses but the diverse array of stalls offering everything from handcrafted Swiss ornaments to delicious local delicacies. At the heart of the market stands a dazzling Christmas tree adorned with thousands of Swarovski crystals, epitomizing the blend of tradition and luxury. It's a sight that captures the spirit of the season, inviting visitors to explore, shop, and indulge.

A short stroll away, you'll find the enchanting Niederdorf Christmas Market, nestled within the charming cobblestone streets of Zurich's Old Town. Here, the atmosphere is a little more intimate, with the stalls offering artisanal goods, local crafts, and delicious Swiss treats. As you wander from stall to stall, vendors warmly share stories of their wares, each piece reflecting Swiss heritage and craft. It's an ideal place to find unique gifts that carry the essence of Zurich back home. The air rings with cheerful chatter and live music, drawing you further into the festive embrace of this quaint locale.

Not to be missed is the Werdmühleplatz Singing Christmas Tree, a quintessential Zurich tradition. This is not just any tree; it doubles as a stage for a choir of local and international talent. Groups clad in festive attire sing classic carols while perched on a multi-tiered platform shaped like a tree, creating a beautiful auditory experience that complements the visual feast. Crowds gather, mulled wine in hand, to join in song or simply enjoy the harmonious sounds that fill the square.

This fusion of music and festivity is irresistible, leaving many with a heartwarming reminder of the season's goodwill.

Zurich's Christmas markets are more than just shopping destinations; they're a culinary journey as well. For those with a passion for food, the markets offer a smorgasbord of flavors that both reflect Swiss tradition and embrace international influences. From the famous Swiss raclette, a cheese lover's delight, melted over fresh potatoes and pickles, to the indulgence of Swiss chocolates and gingerbread, there's something to satiate every palate. Don't overlook the lighter options, like the Brezels and the ubiquitous bratwurst, adding a savory spice to the cool winter air.

The evening is a magical time in Zurich during the Christmas season. As twilight descends, the city is bathed in a warm glow of countless lights. The market stalls glimmer like jewels in the night, and the sound of distant church bells creates an ambiance that's as calming as it is festive. Many visitors find refuge in cozy stalls or nearby cafés, warming themselves with hot cocoa or a classic Swiss Glühwein—spiced wine that promises to melt away the chill of winter.

Take the time to join one of the traditional Christmas tours offered around this time. Guided walks by knowledgeable locals highlight the city's historical backgrounds and the cultural significance of the markets. Travelers get an insider's glimpse into beloved traditions, legends, and the evolution of the Christmas market over the years. These narratives weave a deeper understanding of why Zurich cherishes this time of year so dearly.

Zurich's commitment to sustainability is also evident throughout its Christmas celebrations. Many stalls focus on eco-friendly products, and there's a visible effort to maintain environmental consciousness in both the goods offered and the market operations. This includes using reusable utensils and encouraging visitors to consider sustainable shopping practices. Such conscious efforts ensure that the joy of

Christmas in Zurich doesn't come at the planet's expense, a reminder of the season's underlying message of care and consideration.

Despite Zurich's global reputation as a hub of innovation and finance, during the Christmas period, the city embraces its traditional roots. The harmony between old-world charm and the pulse of modern life offers a unique festive experience, inviting all to partake in its rich holiday tapestry. Whether you're a first-time visitor or a seasoned traveler, Zurich's Christmas markets promise a plethora of memories, each more enchanting than the last.

As you reflect on your visit, you realize that Zurich doesn't just celebrate Christmas—it lives it. The city's markets are a testament to how deeply Zurichers value tradition, community, and the simple joys that make the holiday season truly special. Engaging with the local customs, indulging in the flavors, and soaking in the ambiance offer a passport to the heart of a festive tradition that lingers long after the snow has melted. Zurich's Christmas markets capture not only the essence of the season but also the timeless appeal of sharing warmth and joy in cold winter months.

Lucerne's Lakeside Charm

Lucerne, nestled beside the serene waters of Lake Lucerne and surrounded by the majestic Swiss Alps, is a gem of a city. Known for its picturesque beauty and rich history, this charming town transforms into a magical winter wonderland during the holiday season, offering a unique blend of mesmerizing landscapes and festive traditions. The Christmas market festivities here are unlike anywhere else, capturing both the tranquility of the lake and the grandeur of the snow-capped mountains.

The heart of Lucerne's Christmas celebration can be found in its historic Old Town. Strolling through its cobblestone streets, you'll find yourself surrounded by lovingly decorated wooden stalls, each one a treasure trove of handmade crafts, local delicacies, and festive decorations. As the scents of cinnamon, mulled wine, and roasted nuts fill the air, there's an undeniable warmth that invites travelers and residents alike to indulge in the season's spirit.

Along the lakeside, the Reuss River sparkles under the twinkling lights that frame the Chapel Bridge, one of Lucerne's most iconic landmarks. During the holidays, the bridge itself becomes part of the city's yuletide charm, adorned with twinkling lights that reflect off the tranquil waters below. This stunning display of lights is only the beginning of what the city has to offer. One can't help but pause and take in the breathtaking view of snow-dusted peaks in the distance, merging with the festive ambiance along the shore.

One of the things that set Lucerne apart is its deep commitment to local culture and tradition. The city brings its history to life with events such as the "Klausjagen," a traditional procession held in nearby Küssnacht am Rigi. Participating in such events provides a window into centuries-old customs that continue to thrive in modern Switzerland. These traditions, combined with the city's natural beauty, make the Christmas market experience truly unforgettable.

Various stalls offer artisanal gifts that are perfect for spreading holiday cheer, from hand-knitted scarves to intricate wooden toys. Lucerne's market is an eclectic mix, with influences from across Switzerland coming together. Don't miss out on trying Swiss chocolates, a variety of cheeses, and hearty alpine dishes like rösti, which are sure to warm even the coldest nights.

Beyond the stalls and the culinary delights, Lucerne also offers a series of performances and concerts that set the festive tone. Often, the sounds of choirs and musical ensembles echo through the streets, performing both traditional carols and contemporary holiday tunes. The Culture and Congress Centre Lucerne (KKL) hosts a variety of events, from classical music concerts to avant-garde performances,

Winter Wonderlands

ensuring there's something for every taste. The integration of cultural events with holiday celebrations further enriches Lucerne's lakeside allure.

Venturing slightly further from the main market area, you'll find enchanting spots like the Ice Rink at Inseli Park. Surrounded by glowing Christmas trees and illuminated art installations, this skating experience is fun for families, couples, and anybody with a love for winter sports. Renting a pair of skates to glide over the ice with the glow of the market in the background is a magical experience in itself.

The local community adds to Lucerne's charm by hosting workshops and interactive activities throughout the season. These range from candle-making sessions to cookie-decorating classes, each led by friendly locals eager to share their crafts. Participating in these, even if just for an hour, provides visitors with a deeper connection to the region and its festive spirit.

Lucerne's strategic location makes it an ideal base for excursions into the surrounding mountainous countryside. During the Christmas season, nearby Mount Pilatus turns into a snowy playground, offering thrilling activities like tobogganing, snowshoeing, and winter hiking. For those who prefer a more leisurely exploration, the cogwheel railway provides a stunning ascent to panoramic views that encompass the enchanting beauty of the winter landscape.

As evening falls, the city takes on a dreamy quality. Boats adorned with lights glide silently across the lake, offering holiday cruises with dining and entertainment. As the night sky blankets the city, the lights from these boats create a mirror-like effect on the lake's surface, weaving a tapestry of enchantment.

Lucerne's lakeside charm during the festive season is about more than just the markets and sights. It's an immersive experience where nature, tradition, and community intertwine to create a unique atmosphere of warmth and wonder. As families gather around the comforting glow of stall lights and children play in the picturesque squares, the spirit of the season comes alive in every corner.

It's clear that Lucerne offers a holiday experience that marries tradition and tranquility in an idyllic Alpine setting. The city's Christmas market, bathed in the soft glow of lights and surrounded by the serene beauty of its natural landscape, promises an experience that captivates the senses and warms the heart. Whether you're exploring the historic streets or taking in the majestic views, Lucerne's lakeside charm during the holiday season is a memory waiting to be made.

Chapter 8:
Belgium's Winter Wonders

Stepping into Belgium during the winter season feels like entering a timeless holiday narrative, where cobblestone streets and medieval architecture become the perfect backdrop for festive cheer. While each Belgian city boasts its own unique charm, the magic of Brussels's Grand Place is unparalleled, with its enchanting light show and towering Christmas tree presiding over vibrant market stalls. Just a train ride away, Bruges offers an entirely different yet equally captivating experience, as its medieval markets brim with artisanal crafts and delectable treats that invite visitors to explore at a leisurely pace. Both cities exude a cozy warmth and hospitality that embraces the holiday spirit fully, making Belgium a must-visit destination for those seeking an authentic winter wonderland experience. Let Belgium's blend of history, culture, and festive ambiance inspire you to explore and create heartwarming holiday memories.

Brussels's Grand Place Magic

As you set foot in the heart of Brussels during the festive season, the first thing you'll notice is the ethereal glow of Grand Place. It's as if you've stumbled into a living, breathing postcard, where history and festivity coexist with effortless charm. The square, renowned for its opulent 17th-century architecture, undergoes a metamorphosis each winter. It doesn't merely become a backdrop for the holiday market; it transforms into the market itself—a radiant theater of seasonal joy.

The Grand Place isn't just any square; it's the beating heart of Brussels. Towering guildhalls frame the space with their intricate façades, a testament to elegant Flemish architecture. At Christmastime, lights dance across these historic edifices, painting a stunning tapestry of color and warmth. The focal point of this symphony of lights is the towering Christmas tree, often sourced from the Ardennes forest, a gift from Wallonia. It stands proudly next to a majestic crèche, its life-sized figures telling the timeless nativity story under twinkling starlight.

The magic of Grand Place extends far beyond its visual splendor. The air carries the irresistible aroma of Belgian waffles, simmering chocolate, and spicy mulled wine, inviting you to indulge in the flavors of the season. Vendors populate the square with stalls that brim with artisanal crafts, lovingly created by local artisans. Here, you can find everything from hand-carved wooden toys to delicate lacework, each piece offering a slice of Belgian tradition to take home.

One can't talk about the market without mentioning the nightly sound and light show that transforms the square into a playground of colors. The spectacle captivates audiences with its blend of music and lights, perfectly synchronized to enhance the grandeur of the historical setting. Families, friends, and even solo travelers gaze in awe, wrapped in the universal language of holiday wonder.

Brussels's Grand Place is also a cultural hub of activity during the season. Choirs fill the air with carols, their voices echoing off the guildhalls, creating an atmosphere that feels both intimate and expansive. Street performers add an element of surprise and delight, their acts varying from enchanting to outright whimsical, ensuring that every visit is unique.

Step away from the bustling center of the square, and you'll find the traditional 'Plaisirs d'Hiver'—Winter Wonders—a festival that sprawls over two kilometers throughout the city, but always finds its heart at Grand Place. An ice rink in nearby Marché aux Poissons captures both locals and tourists in its icy embrace, offering an exhilarating diversion from shopping and eating.

For the discerning traveler, Grand Place presents more than just a holiday spectacle. It's an opportunity to engage with the local community. Vendors are eager to share the stories behind their crafts, many of which are steeped in multi-generational family heritage. In every trinket and treat, there's a promise of authenticity, a chance to connect with Belgium's rich cultural tapestry.

It's the sort of place where you live the magic of the moment. Many visitors return year after year, their faces warm with familiarity and anticipation. They seek not just the festive trappings but the indescribable spirit that seems to animate the age-old square—the unexpected sense of belonging in a place so steeped in history, yet so alive in the present.

The experience of Grand Place during the holidays is enduring. It's the kind of encounter that transcends mere tourism, etching itself into your memory with the precision of a master engraver. As you stand there, surrounded by glowing lights and ancient stone, you'll feel the true magic of Brussels underfoot. So, whether it's your first visit or your fiftieth, there's something undeniably enchanting about finding yourself in the Grand Place during the winter season.

Bruges's Medieval Markets

Nestled in a maze of cobblestone streets and surrounded by serene canals, Bruges instantly transports you back in time, especially during the winter season. The city's medieval heart beats strongest when its Christmas markets awaken—a feast for the senses and a retreat to the charm of yesteryears. As snowflakes gently blanket the centuries-old spires, Bruges feels like a scene from a fairy tale, enticing visitors with its unique blend of history and festivity.

As you wander through the town, it's impossible not to notice how the market here stands apart. While many European cities boast markets filled with holiday clichés, Bruges offers something distinctly more authentic. It's a place where tradition reigns, yet the spirit of Christmas is ever vibrant. The city squares, such as the majestic Market Square, are adorned with lights and filled with the inviting scent of roasted chestnuts and mulled wine. Each stall is a quaint wooden hut, showcasing the handiwork of skilled artisans and culinary delights reflective of the region's rich culture.

Bruges's Christmas market isn't merely a shopping destination; it's a cultural experience. Against the backdrop of the Gothic Belfry, visitors line up to sample traditional Belgian waffles, their toasty, sugary aroma mingling with the cool, crisp air. The sound of carolers drifts through the square, weaving a melodic tapestry that you'll carry long after you leave. One can find the warmth of hot chocolate in their hands as they peruse everything from handmade lace to intricate wooden toys.

In Winter Glow, Bruges becomes an illuminated wonderland. This light experience spreads across the city, painting its historic structures with a symphony of colors. The Bruges Ice Sculpture Festival also adds a breathtaking spectacle, where artists transform simple blocks of ice into magnificent displays, from mythical creatures to beloved holiday figures. These events offer an inspiring reminder of the creative soul that beats within this ancient city.

The history of Bruges plays an integral part in the magic of its Christmas markets. Strolling through the narrow streets, it's easy to imagine traders of the Hanseatic League plying their wares in the Middle Ages. Today, that mercantile spirit survives in the warm exchanges over cups of steaming spiced cider found at the market's cozy stalls. Those seeking unique gifts will feel like treasure hunters as they discover hand-crafted jewelry, vibrant ceramics, and textiles that echo centuries of Flemish tradition.

The medieval ambiance of Bruges sets the stage for an enchanting ice rink in Simon Stevin Square. With holiday lights reflecting off the glistening ice, locals and travelers glide gracefully—or not so gracefully—through the brisk winter air, laughter echoing around. It's moments like these that foster a sense of community, where visitors can share in the delight of the season despite differences in language or origin.

A visit to one of Bruges's many artisanal chocolate shops is a must. Belgian chocolate is synonymous with excellence, and Bruges delivers with countless options ranging from the traditional to the inventive. Here, chocolatiers are artists, crafting creations that not only satisfy a sweet tooth but also tell a story of passion and heritage. Each bite of praline or truffle serves as a reminder of the city's dedication to quality and tradition.

The sense of festivity in Bruges extends beyond the markets themselves. Each evening, as the golden light fades, the city's canals mirror the twinkling lights, turning the town into a shimmering, dreamy landscape. On these nights, a simple stroll along the waterways feels magical, with the reflection of the lights dancing on the water's surface, creating an endless dance of joy and cheer.

While Bruges's markets bustle with visitors during the day, there's something equally enchanting about the city after hours. In quiet corners, whispers of history might catch your ear as the streets calm down. Guided evening tours offer an opportunity to delve into the city's past, with tales of its medieval glory days and the characters that once roamed its lanes.

Simply put, Bruges offers a seasonal sanctuary—an escape for those seeking to immerse themselves in the true essence of Christmas.

It doesn't shout for attention but rather invites you to explore its treasures quietly, with curiosity and wonder. Years of history support the weight of tradition, and in every crafted ornament and festive song, you'll find a story waiting to be discovered.

In the heart of Bruges's medieval markets, it's not just about buying gifts or tasting festive treats; it's about embracing a world where past and present mingle effortlessly, creating a tapestry of holiday spirit that envelopes everyone who visits. And as each lantern flickers to life and the city bathes in its glow, you'll realize that the true charm of Bruges lies in its ability to transport you—not just through its historical treasures, but into the very heart of the season itself.

Chapter 9:
Eastern Europe's Yuletide Spirit

As we venture into Eastern Europe's yuletide charm, it's impossible not to be captivated by the region's rich tapestry of beloved traditions and inviting warmth. In cities like Prague, the magic of Christmas comes alive amidst gothic spires and centuries-old squares, where the aroma of mulled wine mingles with the melodic sound of carolers, creating an enchanting atmosphere. Meanwhile, Budapest offers a festive warmth that glows against its historical backdrop, where twinkling lights reflect off the Danube, and vibrant markets invite travelers to explore stalls brimming with handcrafted gifts and local delicacies. As you wander through these wonderlands, the spirit of Eastern Europe's Christmas markets is one of unity and delight, bringing together old and new traditions that echo the region's vibrant past while embracing the festive joy of the present. Through cobblestone streets adorned with festive decor, these markets offer not just shopping, but an immersive experience that celebrates the heart and soul of Eastern Europe during the holiday season.

Prague's Holiday Enchantment

Prague, a city where Gothic spires pierce the winter sky, becomes even more magical during the holidays. As snow blankets its cobbled streets, the Czech capital transforms into a picturesque winter wonderland. It's an enchanting scene straight out of a storybook, where every corner reveals a new facet of festive cheer.

At the heart of this transformation lies the Old Town Square, the focal point of Prague's Christmas celebrations. Here, the majestic Christmas tree stands proud, adorned with thousands of sparkling lights and traditional decorations. This giant sentinel watches over the myriad of stalls that line the square, each offering a glimpse into Czech craftsmanship and culinary delights. It's impossible to resist the allure of handcrafted ornaments that gleam with meticulous detail or the heady aroma of mulled wine that perfumes the frosty air.

The bustle of the marketplace, with its cheerful vendors and eager visitors, adds a warmth to Prague's winter chill. One can't help but be drawn to the tantalizing array of food available. Traditional Czech treats, such as "trdelník," a sweet pastry dusted with sugar and walnuts, tempt both locals and travelers alike. Meanwhile, hearty dishes like "klobása" sausages grilled to perfection provide nourishment against the cold. Every bite offers a taste of Czech tradition and hospitality.

An integral part of Prague's holiday appeal is its vibrant cultural performances. Throughout the city, stages come alive with the sound of carolers, traditional folk dancers, and classical music ensembles. These performances, deeply rooted in Czech culture, captivate audiences, inviting them to become part of the festive spirit. The city's theaters also join in the merriment, presenting seasonal plays and ballets that draw inspiration from Prague's rich artistic heritage.

As night falls, the city shines with a special kind of brilliance. Lights illuminate the historic facades, casting a warm glow on the Charles Bridge and Prague Castle. This mesmerizing spectacle invites visitors to take an evening stroll through the city's illuminated streets, where even familiar landmarks take on a new, ethereal quality.

Beyond the famous Old Town Square, other districts in Prague offer their own unique holiday experiences. The Náměstí Míru square, for instance, hosts a charming yet less-crowded Christmas market, perfect for those seeking a more intimate setting. Surrounded by the stunning architecture of the Church of St. Ludmila, this market features locally-made gifts and serves as a quieter retreat from the bustling city center.

Prague's holiday charm extends even further with traditions that have been passed down through generations. One such tradition is the celebration of St. Nicholas Day. On December 5th, "Mikuláš," along with his companions Angel and Devil, can be seen wandering through the city. This trio delights children with treats and small gifts. It's a charming custom that reflects the playful spirit embedded in Prague's holiday festivities.

For those willing to explore beyond markets and performances, Prague offers a wealth of historical and cultural treasures to enhance the holiday visit. The city's museums and galleries host special exhibitions that offer insight into Czech history and art. Meanwhile, the iconic Prague Castle becomes a canvas of light during the season, with special events that delve into the region's royal past.

Perhaps the most enduring aspect of Prague's holiday enchantment is the city's ability to connect the past with the present. Despite its modern shops and bustling streets, Prague retains an ancient magic that seems amplified during the holiday season. It's a place where time feels both suspended and forward-moving, where the coziness of a traditional café meets the innovative spirit of Czech festive crafts.

The enchantment of Prague during the holidays lies in its ability to bring people together. The city becomes a shared space, a junction where old traditions meet new visitors, and where everyone is welcome to become part of the festive tapestry. As you explore the various facets of Czech culture - from its culinary delights to its age-old customs - you might find that the true charm of Prague lies in its people: warm, welcoming, and always eager to share their stories.

In the end, Prague's magical holiday experience is not merely about visual spectacle or seasonal offerings. It's about a feeling - a deep-seated joy that fills the heart as you walk through its snow-dusted streets and engage with its vibrant traditions. It's a city that, during this special time of year, invites all to embrace its holiday spirit and leave with memories that linger long after the holidays have passed.

Budapest's Festive Warmth

Walking along the streets of Budapest during the holiday season feels like stepping into a scene from a Christmas storybook. The city's captivating beauty, enhanced by a blanket of snow, creates an enchanting backdrop for one of Europe's most inviting Christmas markets. Here, the juxtaposition of the Danube River and historic architecture highlights Budapest's charm, but it's the holiday spirit that truly warms the hearts of its visitors.

At the center of it all is the Budapest Christmas Fair and Winter Festival, held in the picturesque Vörösmarty Square. This market isn't just a place to shop; it's a vibrant gathering of culture, music, and tradition. The square is adorned with twinkling lights and the aroma of cinnamon and mulled wine wafts through the air, drawing in both locals and tourists alike. It's a place where people come together to celebrate the season and create cherished memories.

Divine smells permeate the atmosphere as you explore the festive stalls offering traditional Hungarian delicacies. You can savor foods like "flódni," a rich pastry layered with apples, walnuts, and poppy seeds, or "kürtőskalács," a sweet chimney cake dusted with sugar and cinnamon. Each bite offers a glimpse into Hungary's culinary traditions, ensuring that your taste buds enjoy the holiday as much as your eyes and ears.

The sounds of live music fill the air as local musicians perform beneath the twinkle of festive lights. Traditional folk instruments blend seamlessly with festive carols, creating a heartwarming soundtrack to your market experience. It's impossible not to feel moved by the infectious rhythm and joyful melodies that captivate everyone who listens.

But it isn't just food and music that draw people to this magical corner of Budapest; it's also a mecca for artisans and craftspeople. The stalls, meticulously arranged, showcase an array of handcrafted goods that make perfect holiday gifts. From intricate ornaments to beautifully woven textiles and pottery, each piece tells a story of Hungarian craftsmanship and creativity.

As day turns to night, the market takes on a new level of beauty. The lights twinkle more brightly against the darkened sky, casting a warm, golden glow over the square. Strolling through the market at this time feels almost otherworldly, as if you've been transported to a secret holiday haven. It's easy to get lost in the market's enchantment, with every corner offering a new delight to discover.

The festive atmosphere is amplified by the surrounding architectural beauty of Budapest. Vörösmarty Square, with its majestic buildings and historic sculptures, provides a grand setting that echoes the city's rich past. As you wander through the market, you're reminded of Budapest's unique blend of history and modernity, making it a perfect fit for such a timeless celebration.

For those looking to dive deeper into the festive spirit, the market offers workshops and activities that encourage participation. You can unleash your creativity with gingerbread decorating or learn about traditional crafts like candle-making. These experiences not only entertain but also provide insights into local traditions, enriching your understanding of Hungarian culture.

Another aspect that makes the Budapest Christmas Fair special is its commitment to sustainability and supporting local businesses.

Many vendors focus on eco-friendly practices, offering products made from recycled materials or using sustainable methods. This approach resonates with the growing desire to enjoy the holidays mindfully while supporting local economies.

While Vörösmarty Square is the heart of Budapest's festive celebrations, the spirit of Christmas touches many parts of the city. Various smaller markets pop up in other neighborhoods, each offering a unique slice of local charm. These markets provide a more intimate experience yet maintain the city's warm and inviting holiday spirit.

Visitors also have the opportunity to explore Budapest's famous thermal baths, which offer a perfect escape from the cold winter nights. Submerging in the warm, mineral-rich waters feels like the ultimate indulgence after a day of exploring the markets. It's a chance to relax and rejuvenate while surrounded by the city's historic architecture, a unique fusion of holiday cheer and relaxation.

The heartwarming spirit of Budapest's Christmas markets offers an incredible way to experience the city. The blend of traditional and contemporary influences makes it a standout destination for anyone eager to immerse themselves in Eastern Europe's Yuletide spirit. The memories made in Budapest during this magical season will linger long after the holidays have passed.

Ultimately, Budapest's festive warmth isn't just about the twinkling lights, lively music, or delectable treats—it's about a community coming together to celebrate the holiday season. It's a reminder of the joy that can be found when people gather to share good cheer and celebrate their cultural heritage. As you wander through the enchanting markets and explore the vibrant city, you'll find yourself inspired by the spirit of togetherness that defines Budapest during this special time of year.

Chapter 10:
The Netherlands' Festive Glow

In The Netherlands, the essence of the holiday season radiates through a tapestry of vibrant lights and cherished traditions. The Dutch embrace a sense of gezelligheid, or coziness, as snow-dusted rooftops and twinkling canals set the stage for heartwarming festivities. Strolling through Amsterdam's bustling squares, visitors are greeted with an array of artisanal gifts and aromatic treats that capture the spirit of yuletide cheer. Further south, Maastricht transforms into a dreamlike winter wonderland where the scent of warm Belgian waffles wafts through the air. It's a season of joy, where communities come alive with laughter and music, uniting locals and travelers alike in celebration. As the festive glow of The Netherlands beckons, the echoes of tradition and togetherness light up the darkest nights of the year, inviting all to become a part of this heartwarming spectacle.

Amsterdam's Winter Fun

Amsterdam in winter is a city transformed, adorned with vibrant lights and bustling celebrations. The Dutch capital, known for its picturesque canals and rich cultural history, takes on a festive glow as the holiday season approaches. Amsterdam's charm during this time of year offers an irresistible invitation to wander its cobblestone streets and embrace the winter cheer.

One of the most enchanting experiences in Amsterdam is its array of Christmas markets, where the air buzzes with the aroma of freshly baked stroopwafels and oliebollen, traditional Dutch pastries that seem to have captured the very essence of winter warmth. Stalls brimming with handcrafted goods provide not only perfect gifts but also a glimpse into the craftsmanship that defines Dutch artistry.

Visiting the iconic Museumplein during Christmas is akin to stepping into a winter fairy tale. The square transforms into a bustling ice rink, surrounded by market stalls offering everything from steaming mugs of hot chocolate to beautifully crafted ornaments. Whether a seasoned skater or a hesitant beginner, gliding across the rink with the Rijksmuseum as a backdrop is a must-do experience, offering both thrilling fun and picture-perfect memories.

Venture a little further into the city, and you'll find the Amsterdamsche Kerstmarkt, an annual highlight that captivates locals and tourists alike. Set against the backdrop of the Westergasfabriek, this market is famous for its sustainability and focus on artisanal goods. The atmosphere here is cozy and intimate, with live music performances enhancing the festive spirit while vendors showcase eco-friendly products alongside seasonal treats.

For a more unique holiday treat, Amsterdam offers something truly special: the Light Festival. This festival turns the city's waterways into a mesmerizing gallery of light installations, created by artists from around the world. As you take a boat tour or stroll along the canals, the city is awash with brilliant colors and innovative designs that reflect on the water, creating a magical, dreamlike environment.

Food lovers will find Amsterdam a certain delight during the Christmas season. The winter markets provide a vast array of culinary charms, starting with traditional sausages and crispy fries, served with a variety of sauces. For those with a sweet tooth, Dutch gingerbread and almond-filled speculaas biscuits are a recurrent favorite. Sampling these treats is almost a rite of passage for anyone seeking a true taste of the Netherlands at this festive time.

Amsterdam's local cafés and restaurants also join in the festive celebrations. Many eateries offer special Christmas menus that highlight seasonal and locally-sourced ingredients. It's a chance to indulge in hearty meals that mirror the comfort of the winter months, perhaps paired with a locally brewed craft beer or a warming glass of glühwein, the Dutch version of mulled wine.

The holiday season wouldn't be complete without music, and Amsterdam excels in this cultural aspect as well. Concert halls and churches throughout the city host an array of performances, from classical compositions to modern interpretations of Christmas carols. The Concertgebouw, renowned for its exemplary acoustics, offers a series of holiday concerts that often become the highlight of the season for many visitors.

For families, Amsterdam presents an array of fun activities for all ages. From storytime sessions at the central library, fondly known as the OBA, to craft workshops and puppet shows in various cultural centers, children and adults alike find joy and inspiration at every turn. The city's festive atmosphere provides not only entertainment but also unforgettable family memories.

As the sun sets and the city takes on a shimmering glow, Amsterdam's canals become even more enchanting. A canal cruise is particularly magical in the winter, as twinkling lights reflect off the water, providing a serene and picturesque view of the city. Whether you're bundled up on an open boat or cozy inside a heated cabin, the experience offers a unique perspective of Amsterdam's winter beauty.

A visit to Amsterdam during the winter months wouldn't be complete without exploring the city's array of museums and galleries, many of which host specially curated exhibitions during the holiday season. The Van Gogh Museum, Anne Frank House, or the quirky KattenKabinet offer a cultural respite from the outdoor festivities, embodying the vibrancy and diversity of Amsterdam's rich artistic heritage.

In the midst of the lively celebrations, there is a sense of reflection and community. Amsterdam's winter festivities are not just about extravagance or commercialism but about coming together, celebrating shared traditions, and creating cherished moments. This spirit of togetherness is echoed in the welcoming smiles of locals, who embrace visitors as part of their holiday family.

Amsterdam in winter is not just a destination; it's an experience. The city's blend of historical charm and innovative celebration invites travelers to explore and immerse themselves fully in the festive spirit. Each corner of the city offers something new to discover, a different story to hear, and a unique memory to make, ensuring that winter in Amsterdam is as unforgettable as it is enchanting.

Maastricht's Magical Markets

As shimmering lights adorn the tranquil streets of Maastricht, this Dutch city transforms into a winter wonderland, welcoming visitors to experience its enchanting Christmas markets. Nestled within the heart of Limburg, a region known for its hills and vineyards, Maastricht becomes a captivating blend of Dutch and European festive traditions. You can feel the city's spirit start to shift as the crisp air carries laughter and the soft hum of conversation, echoing through cobblestone streets.

Walking into Maastricht's Magical Markets, your senses are greeted by the familiar yet always thrilling symphony of the holiday season. The scent of warming spices like cinnamon and nutmeg dances through the air, carried by the gentle smoke from countless stalls. Vendors offer freshly baked Stollen, a traditional German fruit bread coated with powdered sugar, alongside other delectable treats like Dutch oliebollen, deep-fried doughnut balls that are a must-try.

Maastricht's market isn't just about the food; it's a feast for the eyes and soul too. The city's main square, the Vrijthof, becomes the center of yuletide festivities, with its neo-Gothic churches providing a stunning backdrop against the twinkling lights. The atmosphere here is infectious, drawing people from all walks of life into its festive embrace. Rows of wooden chalets are adorned with holly and twinkling lights, each one offering unique handmade gifts. From intricately carved wooden toys to artisanal candles, the market celebrates craftsmanship and creativity.

The charm of Maastricht extends beyond the market stalls. An ice skating rink encourages visitors to lace up their skates and glide across the ice under the starry night sky. This isn't just a market; it's an immersive experience that captures the joy of the season. A towering Ferris wheel offers panoramic views of the illuminated city, its colorful lights reflecting off the icy surfaces below, adding to the magical ambiance.

Music plays a crucial role in the Maastricht Christmas Market. Local musicians and choirs fill the air with holiday melodies, ranging from traditional carols to modern festive tunes. These performances make for an enchanting soundtrack as you explore. The Vrijthof stage, a focal point for many cultural performances, often hosts live bands and festive shows, ensuring there's always something to captivate an audience here.

The market's cultural appeal lies not just in its entertainment or goods, but in its history. Maastricht has long been a melting pot of European cultures, positioned at the crossroads of the Netherlands, Belgium, and Germany. This multicultural influence is evident in its festive offerings. Maastricht's market doesn't just aim to replicate its more famous European counterparts; it celebrates its unique position in this cultural triad with pride.

If you're a visitor who treasures culinary exploration, the local street food at the market is an adventure worth embarking on. Dutch specialties such as poffertjes, tiny fluffy pancakes dusted with powdered sugar, provide a sweet delight. Meanwhile, savory options like sausages and cheese—often paired with locally brewed beer—offer a hearty respite from the chill. The experience of tasting these local delicacies, prepared with love and tradition, adds an extra layer to the holiday spirit.

For the history enthusiasts, Maastricht's Christmas Market offers more than just festive enjoyment. Guided tours of the city and its marketplaces often delve into the rich historical tapestry that Maastricht presents year-round. From its Roman roots to its medieval architecture, the city tells a story that enhances the festive ambiance, turning each visit into a journey through time.

Shoppers will find that the Maastricht market caters to a variety of tastes, drawing on local and international influences. Whether you're interested in rare antiques, contemporary crafts, or simply unique gifts for loved ones, there's something special waiting to be discovered. The stalls often feature vintage items, traditional crafts, and modern designs, which means you won't go home empty-handed or uninspired.

As you visit Maastricht's markets, the heartwarming interactions with local vendors create a truly authentic experience. Many artisans are keen to share the stories behind their creations, adding depth and character to your shopping experience. It's these personal touches that turn a simple market visit into a cherished memory, highlighting the communal spirit of holiday celebrations.

For families, the Maastricht Christmas Market is an adventure filled with wonder. Activities for children, such as workshops and storytelling sessions, are plentiful. These interactive experiences help younger visitors connect with the festive traditions of Maastricht, enriching their holiday season with laughter and learning.

To leave the market without a keepsake would be a lost opportunity. Many take home a piece of Maastricht's magic in the form of handcrafted ornaments or locally produced goods. Such mementos serve as beautiful reminders of a journey where past and present unite to celebrate the festive season.

In summary, Maastricht's Magical Markets offer a harmonious blend of tradition, culture, and festive joy. This Dutch city, with its warm-hearted hospitality and enchanting market scene, beckons travelers to come and experience its holiday charm. As you leave, the memories of Maastricht linger long after the last light has faded, and the final bell has rung. Whether visiting for its unique culinary delights, cultural richness, or simply to soak in the festive atmosphere, Maastricht is a holiday destination that inspires and delights at every turn.

Chapter 11:
The Baltic Winter Celebrations

As you wander through the Baltic's snow-dusted streets, you'll find yourself enveloped in a world that beautifully captures the essence of winter celebrations. Tallinn's medieval charm comes to life under twinkling lights, where historic traditions blend seamlessly with modern festivities. In Riga, the bustling Christmas markets entice you with artisanal crafts and aromatic mulled wine, each stall telling its story of festive cheer. The crisp Baltic air carries the sound of holiday music, creating an atmosphere that's cozy yet invigorating. It's in these enchanting cities that the simple joys of the season are celebrated with authenticity and warmth, inviting you to experience the magic of Baltic winter traditions firsthand. From intricate decorations to lively performances, the Baltic region offers a captivating fusion of history, culture, and holiday spirit that promises unforgettable memories.

Tallinn's Timeless Traditions

Each winter, Tallinn transforms into a snow-dusted wonderland, its medieval streets echoing with the warmth of holiday traditions that have been cherished for centuries. From the cobblestone alleys to the magnificent Town Hall Square, the city's festive spirit is palpable, drawing visitors from around the globe. If you're longing for an authentic holiday experience, Tallinn's Christmas market is where you'll find Old World charm coupled with heartwarming traditions.

Winter Wonderlands

The centerpiece of Tallinn's winter celebrations is the grand Christmas tree standing tall in the square. Tallinn proudly claims to be the birthplace of the tradition of decorating a public Christmas tree, dating back to 1441. This includes decking the tree with ornaments that sparkle like stars against a snowy backdrop, a spectacle that warms the hearts of visitors and locals alike. As the winter sun dips below the horizon, the market comes alive with twinkling lights that seem to dance across the crisp night air.

Once you step into the market, your senses are embraced by the smell of mulled wine, rich with spices, weaving through the chilly air. Vendors, bundled up against the cold, offer traditional Estonian fare. One can't help but be drawn to the sizzle of sizzling sausages and the aroma of black pudding, known as verivorst, a local favorite during the holiday season. Each bite offers a taste of Estonian heritage, lovingly preserved through generations.

The market stalls, resembling gingerbread houses dusted with snow, brim with handcrafted goods. Artisans showcase their talents with goods ranging from delicate glass ornaments to woolly mittens, each with detailed intricacies. These are perfect souvenirs, each carrying a story of Estonian craftsmanship and seasonal tradition. Shoppers can also find an array of handmade candles, wooden toys, and unique pottery, ensuring there's no shortage of gift ideas for loved ones back home.

Beyond the towering tree and bustling stalls, Tallinn's holiday traditions expand into the streets, where the sound of carols can be heard from every corner of the city. Choirs and local bands fill the air with melodies that recall Finland's traditional songs, creating a harmonious symphony that overlays the city's cobbled streets. The music acts as a bridge through time, connecting the past with the present as families gather and join in the festivities.

Each day at the market brings new experiences. From storytelling sessions that recount ancient legends to workshops on making traditional Estonian gingerbread, known as piparkoogid, there's something for everyone. These events help visitors dive into the heart of Estonian culture, fostering a deeper appreciation for the country's rich history and festive traditions.

Dancing also plays a significant role in Tallinn's celebrations. Folk dances, performed by groups clad in colorful native costumes, weave stories through movement, capturing the essence of Estonian folklore. These performances are lively and engaging, providing spectators with a cultural tapestry that's as vibrant as it is entertaining. Children take the lead in these dances, laughing joyfully as they twirl around, their excitement matching the jubilation of the season.

Tallinn doesn't only offer thrilling outdoor activities; it provides cozy indoor experiences too. Many visitors seek warmth and cheer in traditional Estonian eateries, where hearty dishes like sauerkraut stew and minced meat pastries grace the tables. These comfort foods, served alongside a hearty mug of warm glög, provide the perfect respite after a frosty day exploring the market.

For those looking to immerse themselves further into Estonian culture, the museums and galleries of Tallinn remain open and welcoming throughout the winter holiday season. Special exhibitions highlight Estonia's history, art, and the continuous evolution of its cultural identity. During the holidays, these cultural institutions add a sprinkle of festive joy by hosting events and workshops tailored for visitors of all ages.

In Tallinn, the enchantment isn't confined to the market. The city's medieval architecture, dusted with a sprinkle of snow, adds an extra layer of magic to the celebrations. The ancient city walls and historic buildings, bathed in the glow of thousands of lights, offer a journey back in time for anyone willing to wander off the beaten path.

Such meandering is best done with a hot drink in hand, like traditional Estonian eggnog or a cup of locally roasted coffee, each sip warming the soul.

Though modernity has ushered in many changes, Tallinn remains grounded in its traditions. The city's ability to blend these cherished customs with contemporary festivities makes it an exceptional destination during the holiday season. Whether you're crafting gifts with local artisans or joining in a spontaneous snowball fight with locals and fellow travelers, Tallinn's charm resonates with everyone who visits.

As you stroll through the market, each delight is a testament to excellence in maintaining timeless traditions while embracing new ideas. The result is an alive bustling atmosphere that charms everyone it reaches, ensuring they return home with fond memories etched in their hearts. Tallinn's timeless traditions may be rooted in history, but they bloom with a vibrancy that ensures they remain relevant through the ages. A winter visit here is not just a trip; it's a journey through time, one that celebrates both nostalgia and renewal.

Riga's Charming Stalls

Step into the heart of Latvia's capital during the chilly embrace of winter, and you'll find Riga transformed into a veritable wonderland, teeming with festive spirit. The city's Christmas market is set against the stunning backdrop of the Old Town, a UNESCO World Heritage site. Here, cobblestone streets guide you through bustling stalls laden with handcrafted treasures and culinary treats. The aroma of spiced mulled wine and freshly baked pastries lures visitors from far and wide, inviting them to indulge in the season's warmth.

Riga's Christmas market, mainly situated in Dome Square, is a sensory delight. Beneath the shadow of the majestic Riga Cathedral, wooden stalls exude a rustic charm, each unique and brimming with handcrafted Latvian goods. Artisans proudly display their creations, from intricate wooden toys to traditional knitted mittens known as "dūraiņi." Buying one isn't just a transaction—it's a piece of living history and craftsmanship passed down through generations.

The market unfolds like a storybook, with each stall offering a new chapter to explore. Colorful garlands and twinkling lights festoon the area, creating an atmosphere ripe with wonder. The sound of festive music melds seamlessly with the laughter of children, who delight in the simple joys of a carousel ride. It's a place where time seems to slow, providing an escape from the hustle and bustle of daily life.

Food stalls are an integral part of Riga's festive allure, offering a variety of traditional treats that promise to satisfy every palate. Don't miss out on trying *piparkūkas*, the fragrant gingerbread cookies that are artfully decorated and perfect with a warm mug of aromatic glögi. For those seeking heartier fare, the market doesn't disappoint—smoked meats, sauerkraut, and black bread are staples that capture the hearty essence of Latvian cuisine.

The market is not just a feast for the senses—it's a feast for the soul. Local folklore comes to life through performances that captivate audiences young and old. It's not uncommon to stumble upon a choir singing traditional Latvian carols, their voices rising into the crisp winter air. These performances are woven into the fabric of the market, offering a cultural dive that extends far beyond mere commercial exchange.

Riga itself is enhanced by the magic of this market. As you wander from stall to stall, the city's history whispers from around every cobbled corner. Consider pausing to admire the iconic Riga Nativity of Christ Cathedral or take a moment to appreciate the stylistic grandeur of the Art Nouveau district. Each landmark tells a part of Riga's rich past, while each festive stall adds to its vibrant present.

No visit to Riga's Christmas extravaganza would be complete without a peek into the craftsmanship of the local artisans. Whether you're searching for intricately carved wooden birds or beautifully woven textiles, the market is a treasure trove for those who appreciate the art of the handmade. Artisans are often eager to share the story behind their creations, offering insights into Latvia's cultural heritage and traditions.

To fully immerse yourself in Riga's festive offerings, consider a guided walking tour that highlights not only the market's wonders but also the city's architectural marvels and rich history. Local guides offer fascinating anecdotes and hidden gems that bring the city to life, making your exploration both informative and enchanting. Whether you're an architecture aficionado or a history buff, there's something in Riga to captivate your interest.

At night, when darkness falls and the temperature dips, the magic truly unfolds. The market glows softly, lit by thousands of fairy lights. It's a time when the whole scene is flecked with a sense of tranquility, where the pace is leisurely, and joy is shared over the clinking of glasses and shared smiles. Chatting with a local vendor or exchanging holiday wishes with a fellow traveler under the sparkling lights can create a sense of community that lingers long after your visit.

Riga's Christmas market is indeed an embodiment of the city's spirit—where history, culture, and celebration intertwine. It's a place to warm your hands, your heart, and your soul, providing an authentic experience filled with both tradition and joy. When you bid farewell to Riga and its charming stalls, you carry with you not just souvenirs, but a piece of Latvia's festive heart—a reminder to return and rekindle your love for this enchanting city.

Chapter 12:
Russia's Winter Extravaganza

Amid the enchanting frost of the Russian winter, Moscow and St. Petersburg unveil a festive season that is nothing short of magical. Moscow's festive squares spring to life with vibrant colors and the cheer of locals and visitors alike, as twinkling lights illuminate the sprawling ice sculptures and meticulously adorned fir trees. Each market stall, amidst the brisk air, offers hearty Russian delicacies and hand-crafted treasures, inviting you to explore the deep cultural richness on every corner. Just a few hundred miles away, St. Petersburg's snowy delights set the stage for a winter wonderland like no other, where historic palaces provide a regal backdrop to festive merriment. Here, under a cascade of snowflakes, the blend of classical music, folk performances, and seasonal treats creates an atmosphere of pure enchantment. Visiting Russia during this time not only lets one partake in the abundance of holiday traditions but also feel the warmth of camaraderie that transcends the chill of the season. This unique experience wraps you in the cozy charm and grand elegance of Russian Christmas celebrations, compelling even the most seasoned traveler to wander these festive sites with a heart full of wonder and joy.

Moscow's Festive Squares

Moscow in winter transforms into a mesmerizing wonderland, where the festive spirit embraces every corner with its snowy charm and vibrant lights. It's not just the change in weather that makes this city shine bright, but the way it embraces the holiday season with full-hearted zeal. The city squares are alive with a unique blend of Russian tradition and modern festivities, inviting travelers to bask in their celebratory glow.

Red Square, the heart of Moscow, is where the magic begins. Beneath the shadow of the Kremlin and the colorful domes of St. Basil's Cathedral, the square hosts a Christmas market that feels almost otherworldly. Here, the ancient and the contemporary merge amid the hushed tones of falling snow, drawing locals and visitors alike to experience something truly special. Rows of charming wooden stalls line the square, each adorned with twinkling fairy lights and offering a splendid array of handcrafted Russian gifts, from intricately painted matryoshka dolls to luxurious hand-knit shawls.

In these bustling aisles, the scent of mulled wine and roasted chestnuts beckons, wrapping you in warmth despite the chilly air. As you wander further, the melodies of traditional Russian carols fill the square, performed by choirs nestled in quaint kiosks. The festive energy is contagious, pulling everyone into a shared rhythm of joy and celebration. Even amidst the throng, there's a sense of intimacy, a feeling that you're part of something both grand and personal.

The ice rink at Red Square is another highlight, where skaters glide elegantly under a canopy of vibrant lights. Whether you're an expert or a novice, joining them on the ice is a delightful way to immerse yourself in the festive atmosphere. Around you, the laughter of friends and families rings out, echoing against the storied walls of the Kremlin. It's more than just an activity; it's a moment to savor the joyful camaraderie that defines the Russian holiday spirit.

GUM, Moscow's historic shopping arcade, stands majestically along Red Square, acting both as a shopping haven and a festive display. During this season, GUM's aisles are transformed with extravagant decorations; its halls decked with strings of lights, enormous ornaments, and typically Russian festive decorations. Here, the sense of luxury meets nostalgia, as high-end stores offer exclusive holiday collections alongside charming pop-up stalls selling traditional holiday fare.

Venturing away from Red Square, other parts of the city invite discovery. Manezhnaya Square, just a stone's throw away, hosts one of Moscow's most delightful Christmas villages. Visited by numerous tourists and Muscovites, this square offers a less crowded but equally enchanting holiday experience. The market makes strides to present everything local, filled with artisan crafts and culinary wonders. Wherever you turn, there are tempting delights: blinis topped with sour cream and caviar, pelmeni steaming hot from cauldron-like pots, and pirozhki fresh from the oven, each bite a taste of authentic Russian holiday fare.

The festive air in Moscow is not confined to nightfall, as daytime offers its own enchantments. It may be less illuminated, but the charm remains palpable. Children's laughter resonates at dedicated family zones, where interactive performances and storybook characters captivate young visitors. These moments weave a magic of their own, bringing smiles that light up frostblushed cheeks.

For travelers, Moscow's festive squares offer an authentic dive into Russian culture, seamlessly blending the old with the new. It's a place where history breathes through every cobblestone and tradition hangs in the frosty air. Each square holds its own tale and charm, inviting exploration and appreciation. The city's architectural grandeur and cultural richness serve as a breathtaking backdrop to festivities that seem both exotic and familiar.

As twilight descends, Moscow's festive squares take on another aspect of romantic charm. The glowing lights reflect off the snow, giving the entire cityscape a soft, ethereal aura. Walking through these illuminated avenues, hand-in-hand with a loved one or sharing laughter with friends, creates memories that linger long after the snow melts away.

There's an undeniable allure in the contrast of Moscow's historic monuments against the fresh vibrancy of holiday decor. Wrapped in the warmth of its welcome, you find more than a market; you discover a sense of belonging and wonder. Moscow's festive squares encapsulate the spirit of the season, urging you to move beyond mere exploration and into heartfelt experience.

In this city where past and present dance in celebration, the festive squares are invitations—to see, to taste, to hear, and to feel the profound joy of the Russian winter. Therein lies the true extravaganza: the unity of tradition and festivity nestled within the cold embrace of Moscow's wintry charm.

St. Petersburg's Snowy Delights

Imagine stepping into a winter wonderland where history, culture, and the magic of the holiday season intertwine seamlessly. That's precisely what St. Petersburg offers travelers during its enchanting winter months. Known for its imperial past and baroque architecture, this city transforms into a landscape straight out of a fairy tale when covered in a blanket of snow. It's not just about the architectural grandeur, though; it's the spirit of celebration that engulfs the city, turning every corner into a festive spectacle.

The heart of St. Petersburg's festive charm lies in its Christmas markets. Not many might associate Russia with such markets, given its Orthodox tradition which celebrates Christmas later than the Western world. However, these markets have become a melting pot of cultural traditions, blending Russian winter celebrations with Western holiday elements. The markets are adorned with twinkling lights and colorful decorations, resembling a Christmas card come to life. Vendors set up stalls offering everything from handcrafted ornaments to exquisite Russian dolls, making it a perfect haven for unique gift shopping.

One of the most captivating features of St. Petersburg's markets is the culinary offerings, which provide a mouthwatering introduction to the local cuisine. Stroll through the stalls and you're likely to find traditional Russian foods like *blini* (thin pancakes) and *pelmeni* (dumplings), often served with steaming hot mulled wine or fragrant tea to ward off the cold. There's something undeniably comforting about holding a warm mug while wandering under the dazzling fairy lights and the frosty mist of the night.

If St. Petersburg shines during the day, it positively shimmers at night. As the sun dips below the horizon, the city's landmarks are bathed in the glow of festive lights. Nevskiy Prospekt, the city's main artery, becomes a mesmerizing tableau of illuminations that captivates visitors and locals alike. Market squares host live performances and carolers, creating an atmosphere of joy that rings through the air, inviting everyone to join the merriment.

The Christmas markets in St. Petersburg offer more than just shopping. They are cultural events that celebrate the city's rich heritage with music, dance, and theater performances. Ice sculptures dominate many spaces, showcasing the artistic prowess synonymous with Russian craftsmanship. It's not uncommon to come across ice skating rinks right within the markets, where you can glide gracefully—or attempt to—amidst the festive hustle and bustle.

No visit to St. Petersburg would be complete without exploring its historical landmarks, which look even more picturesque under a dusting of snow. The Hermitage Museum, one of the largest and most prestigious museums in the world, offers a journey through art and history that feels fitting in this city of grandeur. Nearby, the Church of the Savior on Spilled Blood stands out with its colorful onion domes, seemingly more vibrant against the stark white of winter.

Visitors may find themselves captivated by the Mariinsky Theatre, home to many renowned ballet and opera performances. The artistry reaches new heights during the winter season, with seasonal performances that pay tribute to the rich traditions of Russian culture. It's an opportunity to delve into the artistic heart of the city, where every performance weaves tales of old into the fibers of the present celebrations.

For those looking to explore beyond the bustling markets and theaters, St. Petersburg offers a variety of winter activities. Take a sleigh ride through the city's parks or along the frozen rivers, where the sound of bells jingling is the perfect soundtrack to the scenic views of snow-covered landscapes. Alternatively, a walk through the city's gardens provides a tranquil escape, where the beauty of nature is set against the backdrop of the wintry cityscape.

In St. Petersburg, the pace of life seems to slow, allowing you to truly savor each moment. Whether gliding on ice or sipping something warm by a fire, the city invites you to embrace its winter charm. While it may be a place deeply rooted in its storied past, St. Petersburg's holiday spirit is undeniably contemporary, blending time-honored traditions with the vibrancy of modern festivities.

Ultimately, the snowy delights of St. Petersburg are more than just visual treats; they are a sensory and cultural journey that beckons travelers to experience the essence of a Russian winter. As you wander through its illuminated streets and listen to the gentle hum of festive melodies, you'll find that St. Petersburg doesn't just celebrate the holiday season—it embodies it. This city, with its unique blend of elegance and warmth, reminds us that sometimes, the true delight of winter lies in embracing the experiences that each snowflake brings.

St. Petersburg's ability to blend its formidable history with contemporary holiday festivities makes it a must-see during the winter months. As the city embraces its snowy transformation, it offers visitors an opportunity to step into a world where past, present, and future meet, creating memories that promise to linger well beyond the festive season. Whether you're meandering through a vibrant market, skating under twinkling lights, or sipping something warm while admiring the snow, St. Petersburg promises unparalleled winter magic. This Russian jewel indeed shines the brightest when dressed in winter's frosty gown, inviting all who visit to partake in its enchanting charm.

Chapter 13:
The Danube Region's Seasonal Charm

As you journey along the majestic Danube, the allure of its Christmas markets captivates with a blend of tradition and modernity found nowhere else. This region becomes a festive wonderland during the winter months, with twinkling lights and charming stalls lining the riverbanks from Vienna to Budapest. It's the season's magic woven into the very fabric of each town, where traditions come alive amidst a backdrop of historical architecture and scenic landscapes. Music fills the air, echoing the rich cultural tapestry of the region as visitors savor the aromas of mulled wine and freshly baked pastries. The Danube's seasonal charm lies not just in its picturesque markets but in the timeless stories of connection and celebration shared by those who meander through its enchanting streets. Whether you're exploring Vienna's elegant squares filled with jubilant carolers or Budapest's bustling riverside, this chapter invites you to embrace the festive spirit and discover the heartwarming vitality of the Danube's holiday charm.

Vienna to Bratislava's Twin Celebrations

The Danube River, a timeless waterway weaving through Europe's heart, offers a unique canvas for holiday celebrations, where tradition meets modernity against a backdrop of twinkling lights and snowy streets. From Vienna to Bratislava, this stretch of the Danube is a tapestry of merry sounds, delectable scents, and vibrant sights. Here, two cities join hands in a festive embrace, showcasing their own distinctive charms yet united in the spirit of the season.

Vienna, the Austrian capital, stands majestically along the Danube, enchanting visitors with its ethereal Christmas markets. Picture baroque streets lined with wooden huts adorned with garlands and shimmering baubles. The city's historic Rathausplatz becomes a wonderland, where the air is heavy with the scent of Glühwein and roasted chestnuts. This market, much like Vienna itself, is a harmonious blend of elegance and festivity.

Strolling through Vienna during the holiday season, you can't help but admire the craftsmanship of local artisans. Intricately carved ornaments, hand-knitted winter wear, and traditional toys — each item tells a story of Austria's rich cultural heritage. On cold winter nights, locals and tourists alike gather, indulging in a glass of mulled wine, the warmth of which spreads not just through the body but the soul.

But it's not just the markets that capture the spirit of Vienna. The city lights up with concerts, quaint ice skating rinks, and nativity scenes. Vienna's musical heritage comes alive with harmonious choirs echoing through the main squares. These musical interludes bring an ethereal quality to the bustling markets and streets, making them feel almost otherworldly.

A snow-capped train ride along the Danube unveils the eventual arrival into Bratislava, Slovakia's charming capital, where a different yet complementary kind of magic awaits. The journey itself is a transition, a scenic glide from Vienna's imperial grandeur to Bratislava's quaint charm. As the festive lights of Bratislava come into view, an anticipation builds — a promise of yet more seasonal delights.

Bratislava's markets, though smaller than those of its Austrian neighbor, are brimming with warmth and a sense of community. The

Main Square market is the heart of the city's celebrations, an intimate space where stalls spill over with local delicacies like Lokše and mead. Here, the vibe is as friendly as the prices, making it a beloved spot for travelers seeking authenticity without the throngs.

Wandering through Bratislava, one can sense a hint of nostalgia mingled with the festive excitement. The city's medieval architecture is the perfect backdrop for twinkling lights and carol singers, creating a postcard-worthy scene at every corner. The Old Town Hall transforms into a cheerful hub, its tower overseeing Bratislava's festive spirit.

These festive twin cities, though separated by a fifty-mile stretch of the river, share more than just geography. Both Vienna and Bratislava offer a glimpse into the region's soulful celebrations, where history is a dancer in the masquerade of lights and laughter that the markets bring. Traditions in both cities are carefully preserved yet joyously presented — an embodiment of the season's goodwill and camaraderie.

For those who seek adventure beyond the markets, the Danube's embrace extends opportunities for river cruises, providing unparalleled views of both capitals in their holiday finery. Twilight descends softly, casting a spell even as the sun dips below the horizon and the markets become illuminated diamonds against the velvet night.

The fusion of historic elegance with delightful festivities in Vienna and Bratislava creates an atmosphere that is nothing short of magical. Visitors find themselves caught up in a flow, much like the Danube itself, meandering through moments of joy, melody, and flavor. It's easy to lose oneself entirely, succumbing to the charm these cities exude in tandem, each offering its unique reflection on the water of the holiday spirit they so proudly share.

These twin celebrations invite travelers to traverse realms of cultural richness, where they can savor delicacies, revel in traditions, and carry the warmth of human connection. Visit Vienna and

Bratislava during the holiday season, and you're not just a visitor; you're part of the grand tableau of celebration.

While Vienna and Bratislava are distinct in their expressions of holiday cheer, the Danube down their middle is ever-persistent in its role as a bridge — a bridge joining not only land but hearts during this most treasured time of year.

Budapest's Riverside Markets

Perched along the banks of the majestic Danube River, Budapest's Riverside Markets are a visual and sensory delight, blending centuries-old traditions with contemporary flair. The city's unique location, straddling the river and combining the historic grandeur of Buda with the vibrant culture of Pest, makes it a truly enchanting Christmas destination. Illuminated by a canopy of lights, the markets stretch along the riverfront, creating a magical atmosphere where the spirit of the season is palpable. The outdoor stalls, filled with holiday goodies and festive decorations, invite visitors to wander and explore at their leisure. It's a place where one can truly experience the warmth of Hungarian hospitality amidst the crisp winter air.

The Riverside Markets cater to both locals and tourists, offering a blend of traditional Hungarian crafts and modern creations. Stalls brimming with handcrafted ornaments and intricate lacework offer a glimpse into the country's rich artisanal history. Visitors can't resist picking up unique Christmas decorations, perfect as mementos of their Budapest adventure. A stroll through these markets is much more than a shopping expedition. It's an immersive cultural experience where the past meets the present, and every glance reveals something new and delightful.

Food plays a central role in Budapest's Riverside Markets. The savory aromas of chimney cakes and goulash permeate the air, luring visitors from stall to stall. Hungarians take immense pride in their

Winter Wonderlands

culinary heritage, and these markets are a testament to that passion. You'll find yourself irresistibly drawn to the Kürtőskalács stands, where this sweet, spiraled pastry is grilled over open flames and generously coated in cinnamon or powdered sugar. For those with a heartier appetite, a steaming bowl of gulyás, Hungary's signature dish, provides the perfect antidote to the crisp winter chill. Every bite tells a story, interweaving the flavors of the nation with the warmth of the festive season.

Beyond the food and crafts, the markets at Budapest also celebrate music and performance, with stages scattered throughout featuring live concerts and traditional folk dances. The soulful sound of carolers fills the air, their voices echoing along the riverbank, fostering a deeper connection between visitors and the holiday spirit. The vibrant performances highlight Hungary's rich musical legacy, drawing crowds into impromptu dance circles and fostering a sense of community and joy.

The Budapest Riverside Markets aren't just about the festive bustle. They offer moments of quiet reflection and awe. Perhaps you'll take a pause by the riverbank, watching as the city lights reflect off the Danube's surface, each ripple carrying a flicker of holiday magic. The beauty of the surroundings is a gentle reminder of the joy that simplicity and nature bring, even amidst the most decorated of holiday settings. There's a tranquil comfort in watching couples and families glide by on the nearby ice-skating rink, their laughter blending with the city's soft hum.

As day transitions into night, Budapest offers a spectacle of lights that transform the Riverside Markets into an illuminated wonderland. Bridges like the Széchenyi Chain Bridge, adorned with twinkling lights, form a picturesque backdrop, their gentle arches framing the market scene. With festive projections on historic buildings and illuminated trees casting a warm glow, Budapest offers a visual feast that captivates all who visit, enveloping them in its unique holiday charm.

Attending the Budapest Riverside Markets is more than an exploration of the markets themselves. It's an opportunity to delve deeper into Budapest's history, with proximity to landmarks such as the Parliament Building and Buda Castle. Within walking distance, these iconic sites offer visitors a chance to interlace their holiday experience with a touch of the city's storied past. It's in moments like these that the markets' true charm is revealed, intertwining the cultural tapestry of Hungary with the festive spirit.

In summary, Budapest's Riverside Markets unveil the true essence of the Danube Region's seasonal charm. It's a place where tradition, culture, and modernity blend seamlessly, creating an unforgettable Yuletide experience. With every step, the festive aura envelops you, drawing you into a celebration that reaffirms the joy of festive exploration. The riverside setting is integral to the allure, offering panoramic views that complement the animated market environment, making it a must-visit for anyone seeking the ultimate Christmas market experience.

Chapter 14:
Poland's Holiday Heritage

Poland's holiday markets offer an enchanting blend of history and tradition woven into the festive fabric of its cities. Amidst the cobbled streets of Krakow and the bustling squares of Warsaw, the spirit of Christmas comes alive with a delightful mix of sights, sounds, and scents. Visitors can wander among charming wooden stalls filled with artisanal gifts and mouth-watering local delicacies, such as pierogies and gingerbread. The crisp winter air carries the sound of carolers, while twinkling lights cast a magical glow over historic architecture. This festive atmosphere does more than just warm the heart; it invites explorers to step into a world where age-old customs meet the joy of modern celebrations. For those with a thirst for rich cultural experiences, Poland's markets promise both nostalgia and novelty, making them an unforgettable highlight of the holiday season.

Krakow's Medieval Magic

Krakow, the historic heart of Poland, offers a captivating Christmas experience that feels like stepping back in time. The city, rich in medieval architecture and history, truly embraces the holiday spirit. Walking through the renowned Main Market Square, you're instantly enveloped in an atmosphere where old-world charm meets festive cheer. With its Gothic churches and cobblestone streets, Krakow becomes a winter wonderland, offering not just a market, but a magical experience.

The Main Market Square, or Rynek Główny, is itself a marvel—one of Europe's largest medieval town squares. This expansive space transforms into a vibrant hub of holiday activity each December. Under a canopy of sparkling lights, vendors display their wares in charming wooden stalls. There is an air of genuine warmth and hospitality as locals and visitors mingle, seeking out the perfect Christmas gifts amongst the handcrafted goods.

One of the most alluring aspects of Krakow's Christmas market is its strong roots in Polish traditions. Here, you can admire beautiful hand-carved wooden toys, exquisite ornaments, and intricate glassware crafted by artisans whose skills have been passed down through generations. The market not only celebrates the festive season but also highlights Poland's rich cultural heritage.

Food, of course, is at the heart of any Polish celebration, and Krakow's Christmas market is no exception. The air is filled with the mouthwatering aromas of local delicacies. You might find yourself drawn to a stand selling pierogi, savory dumplings filled with cheese, potatoes, or meat, and a quintessential Polish dish. Alongside these are the famous smoked sausages, grilled to perfection. Sweet treats like gingerbread and oscypek, a traditional smoked cheese, offer the perfect balance to the hearty, savory options.

For those looking to warm their spirits against the crisp winter air, a cup of Grzaniec—the Polish version of mulled wine—does just the trick. Infused with spices like cinnamon and clove, it's not only delicious but also serves as a toasty hand warmer while you continue your exploration of the market.

Music plays a vital role in enriching the market atmosphere. Traditional carolers often fill the air with seasonal melodies, drawing visitors into the collective joy of the season. Local choirs sometimes perform, sharing the beauty of Polish Christmas songs, bridging language barriers and inviting all to join in the celebration, if only by tapping a foot or humming along.

Krakow's medieval spirit isn't confined to the market alone. Nearby, architectural gems such as St. Mary's Basilica loom beautifully over the square, their facades lit up, adding to the enchantment. Each hour is marked by the playing of the Hejnał Mariacki, a traditional bugle call, from the Basilica's tower—a tradition steeped in history that resonates deeply during the Christmas season.

Venturing beyond the square, visitors can explore Krakow's historical old town, which retains its medieval layout and charm. Festive decorations adorn the streets, leading curious wanderers past historic sites like the Wawel Castle and through quaint alleyways. This is a city where every corner offers a new story, a new piece of history revealed by the gentle fall of snow.

What truly sets Krakow's Christmas market apart is its ability to merge past and present seamlessly. It's a place where time-honored customs exist alongside modern influences, creating an experience that is both nostalgic and refreshing. For the holiday enthusiast, this blend of old and new provides a deeper connection to the spirit of Christmas, radiating warmth even on the coldest winter day.

The quiet beauty of Krakow during the holiday season encourages reflection and appreciation of life's simpler pleasures. As you walk through the market, sipping on warming drinks and taking in the lively atmosphere, there's a sense of belonging and peace. It's a reminder of the universal bonds that connect people, regardless of where they come from.

For those inspired by history and culture, Krakow offers a unique view of how these elements shape and enrich holiday traditions. In this city, the holiday market becomes more than just a shopping destination. It transforms into a living tapestry of Poland's vibrant heritage, inviting everyone to find their place within its story.

As the day winds to a close and the market stalls begin to dim, the festive energy lingers. The soft glow of streetlights reflects off the snow-cloaked cobblestones, and the church bells ring out, echoing across the night. In Krakow, the magic of a medieval Christmas isn't just something to witness; it's an invitation to immerse oneself in the heart of holiday wonder and discover a piece of Poland's soul.

Warsaw's Winter Wonderland

As the chill of winter envelopes Poland, Warsaw transforms into a spectacular winter wonderland, offering a captivating blend of history and festivity. Nestled in the heart of the city, the Warsaw Christmas Market emerges as a beacon of holiday cheer. With its roots deeply intertwined in Polish culture, this market dazzles both locals and visitors with its vibrant atmosphere and rich traditions.

Located in the beautifully restored Old Town Square, Warsaw's Christmas Market stands as a testament to the resilience and spirit of the city. The square, with its cobblestone streets and pastel-colored facades, provides a charming backdrop that enhances the feeling of stepping into a holiday postcard. It's almost as if time slows down here, letting visitors savor each festive moment.

Stalls line the square, their wooden structures adorned with twinkling lights and aromatic garlands. These stalls are a treasure trove of traditional goods and local crafts, offering everything from hand-painted ornaments to intricate lacework. For those seeking unique holiday gifts, the market is a paradise. One can find hand-carved wooden toys, gleaming with the craftsmanship of artisans who have honed their skills over generations.

Beyond the material, Warsaw's Christmas Market is an olfactory delight. The scent of mulled wine, known locally as "grzaniec," beckons from numerous stalls. Each warm sip of this spiced beverage soothes the winter chill, infusing visitors with a sense of warmth and celebration. Alongside, the enticing aroma of freshly made pierogi fills the air. These delicious dumplings, often stuffed with savory fillings like mushrooms and cabbage, provide a comforting taste of Poland's culinary heritage.

Throughout the market, joyful sounds of carolers echo, their melodies narrating tales of yule and joy. Traditional Polish Christmas carols, or "kolędy," play a pivotal role in the festivities. Listening to these songs, one can't help but feel enveloped by the spirit of the season, shared and cherished by generations of Poles.

Children's eyes light up as they catch sight of the market's many attractions. An ice rink glistens nearby, inviting young and old alike to glide across its surface under the twinkling night sky. Laughter and the sound of skates cutting across ice create an atmosphere of joy. Nearby, a carousel, adorned with festive lights and charming characters, spins merrily, offering a whimsical escape for the little ones.

Moreover, Warsaw's winter charm extends beyond the market stalls. The entire city dons its festive attire, with streets illuminated by dazzling displays. Public squares feature grand Christmas trees, their towering form a central piece of the yuletide decor. Walking through the streets, one encounters various installations and lights, each more intricate than the last, turning the city into a canvas of holiday artistry.

While the festivities are delightful in their essence, the true magic of Warsaw's winter wonderland lies in its cultural celebrations. Traditional Polish customs come alive during this season, offering visitors insight into the country's rich heritage. "Gwiazdka," the Polish Christmas Eve, holds special significance, marked by a family gathering and a hearty feast. Markets often feature displays depicting a traditional Polish Christmas dinner, showcasing iconic dishes like "barszcz" (beet soup) and "uszka" (dumplings).

There's also a strong sense of community that resonates through the market. Locals and visitors alike come together in shared celebration, breaking through language barriers with smiles and gestures of goodwill. These moments of connection, forged through shared laughter and stories, embody the spirit of the Polish holiday season as much as any ornament or stall.

As snow gently falls upon Warsaw, covering rooftops and cobblestones in a pristine blanket, it becomes clear why this market is cherished. It's not just about the sights, sounds, or even the tastes. It's about an experience that blends old-world charm with contemporary celebration, capturing the heart and soul of Polish winter traditions.

In Warsaw, the holiday season is not merely a celebration, but an embodiment of the resilience and joy that defines this historic city. This blend of the old and new, tradition and modern festivity, ensures that visitors leave not just with souvenirs, but with cherished memories and perhaps an invitation to return and experience it all over again.

Chapter 15:
The Balkan's Festive Spirit

In the heart of the Balkans, the festive season bursts forth with a unique vibrancy that blends age-old customs with seaside charm. As December arrives, Croatia's coastal towns transform their ancient squares into winter wonderlands, where the salty sea breeze mixes with the aroma of mulled wine and roasted chestnuts. Strings of twinkling lights illuminate the cobblestone streets, guiding visitors to artisan stalls brimming with intricate handicrafts and toasty treats. Not far away, Serbia captivates with its exuberant festivities, where traditional music and dance are as much a part of the celebration as the hearty, soul-warming cuisine. Here, locals and travelers come together to revel in the warmth of community spirit, making these markets not just places to shop, but destinations to experience the true essence of Balkan hospitality during the holiday season. The festive spirit in this region is as hearty as a Serbian feast and as welcoming as a Croatian hug, inviting all to enjoy the season's magic like nowhere else.

Croatia's Coastal Celebrations

Croatia's coastline, renowned for its stunning Adriatic backdrop and charming towns, transforms into a festive wonderland during the holiday season. As you wander through its bustling Christmas markets, the salt of the sea mingling with the scent of mulled wine, you'll find a celebration of both tradition and spectacle that captures the essence of Croatia's coastal spirit. The combination of historical architecture, lively festivities, and vibrant traditions makes Croatia's coastal celebrations a unique and enchanting experience.

Picture the sun setting over the Dalmatian coast, where the golden hues of the sky gently blend into the deep blues of the Adriatic Sea. Here, the cobblestoned streets of cities like Split and Dubrovnik become alive with twinkling lights and the joyful hum of Christmas music. These coastal gems offer a distinct festive flair, pulling you into a cultural tapestry rich with history and tradition. The Christmas markets, perched along seafront promenades and nestled within ancient city walls, invite locals and visitors alike to savor not just the sights, but the spirit of the season.

In Split, the spirit of Christmas envelops the iconic Diocletian's Palace. The ancient Roman fortress turns into a vibrant venue for holiday festivities, where tradition meets modernity with striking grace. Locals and tourists stroll among stalls brimming with handcrafted goods, candles, and festive decor. The melodies of Christmas carols echo off the stone walls, joining the laughter of families enjoying the cheerful atmosphere. With each step, the warmth of Croatian hospitality becomes palpable, inviting you to partake in this delightful immersion into holiday cheer.

Dubrovnik, with its picturesque old town framed by medieval walls, offers a slightly different yet equally captivating experience. As the city streets glow with decorative lights, local artisans showcase their crafts—intricately woven textiles, unique jewelry, and traditional holiday ornaments. The aroma of "fritule," small Croatian doughnuts, fills the air, their sweet scent a call to savor the local flavors of the festive season. These treats pair beautifully with a glass of "rakija," the traditional Croatian brandy, offering a taste of local culinary traditions that warm the soul in chilly December breezes.

In coastal celebrations, the heart of Croatian Christmas traditions beats strongly through music, dance, and communal gatherings. Folk groups, dressed in traditional attire, perform dance renditions passed down through generations, their vibrant rhythms inviting onlookers to join the revelry. Seasonal concerts held in historical venues offer a touch of elegance and a unique soundscape, blending classical and holiday music in a setting steeped in history. The sound of harmonized voices, enhanced by stunning acoustics, accompanies the glow of candlelight, creating moments of pure enchantment.

The smaller coastal towns, often overlooked outside of the summer months, reveal their hidden charm during the holiday season. Town squares become the focal points of community life, adorned with festive decorations and a cheerful bustle. In places like Zadar and Šibenik, local stories and legends come alive in nativity scenes and storytelling sessions that engage both young and old. These communal festivities foster a sense of togetherness and belonging, reminding everyone of the shared joy Christmas brings.

A short ferry ride takes you to the islands like Hvar and Korčula, each offering its distinctive take on Christmas charm. On Hvar, known for its lavender fields and azure waters, the holiday markets celebrate local craftsmanship and gastronomy. You can indulge in homemade sausages, cheeses, and desserts while browsing stalls for unique gifts. Meanwhile, Korčula revives its own historical pageantry with winter festivities that echo the island's legendary Moštra dance, an epic storytelling tradition that captivates audiences with its dynamic performance against a backdrop of holiday lights.

Croatia's coastal celebrations also serve as a reminder of the importance of preserving traditions while embracing contemporary influences. Young artisans innovate, combining traditional techniques with modern designs, creating a dynamic blend of old and new. At the same time, technology and social media bring global attention to these local celebrations, adding a fresh dimension to well-loved customs. This fusion of tradition and modernity ensures that Croatia's festive spirit continuously evolves, offering new experiences for generations to come.

The allure of Croatia's coastal Christmas extends beyond the markets and festivities. Visitors often find themselves enchanted by the natural beauty that serves as a backdrop to these celebrations. From the tranquil fjords of Kotor Bay to the idyllic beaches dusted with a rare winter frost, the country offers breathtaking vistas. A morning stroll by the sea, with the distant sound of gulls and the gentle crash of waves, pairs perfectly with an afternoon of festive indulgence, creating memories that last well after the holiday season ends.

In essence, Croatia's coastal celebrations are an invitation to experience a Christmas that resonates with warmth, community, and joy. It's about cherishing traditions while savoring the unique blend of cultures that define the Adriatic coast. Whether you're warming your hands with a hot cup of local spiced cider under a canopy of stars or joining in a traditional dance in a lively square, Croatia offers a Christmas experience that feels both wonderfully familiar and exhilaratingly new. The coastal celebrations leave a lasting impact, filled with cherished memories that embody the heart of the holiday season.

Serbia's Vibrant Traditions

Serbia, a country cradled in the heart of the Balkans, is home to some of the most vibrant and deeply rooted holiday traditions in Eastern Europe. With a rich tapestry of cultural influences, the festive season here is a harmonious blend of ancient Slavic customs, Orthodox Christian rituals, and modern-day celebrations, creating an intoxicating mix for any traveler eager to dive into a unique holiday experience. As the first snowflakes touch the cobblestone streets of Belgrade's charming squares or the quaint villages nestle under a blanket of white, Serbia comes alive with a festive spirit that is both authentic and heartwarming.

In Serbia, Christmas is celebrated on January 7th, following the Julian calendar. This date sets the tone for a season that feels delightfully extended compared to the more widely celebrated December 25th. The anticipation builds over weeks, with festive markets opening long before Christmas day. Towns and cities across Serbia light up with decorations, and the air fills with the inviting aromas of mulled wine, roasted chestnuts, and specijaliteti—delicious local specialties that lure both locals and tourists to the vibrant market stalls.

Belgrade holds a special place in the heart of Serbia's festive map. The capital is renowned for its lively Christmas markets that pop up in its central squares, blending Serbian traditions with a modern twist. Republic Square transforms into a winter wonderland, where locals and visitors alike can browse gifts and handicrafts. Stalls line the streets, offering traditional Serbian food from warm, flaky pastries known as 'pita,' to spicy sausages known as 'kobasice,' giving a warm escape from the chilly weather.

Visiting one of these markets is like stepping into a festive storybook. The rhythmic beats of traditional folk music provide the soundtrack to the backdrop of twinkling lights. Street performers, adorned in colorful costumes, dance and sing, adding to the joyful atmosphere. It's easy to get swept up in the revelry, joining in a kolo, the local circle dance, which is a staple at numerous festivities throughout the season.

A journey through Serbia during the holiday season wouldn't be complete without exploring its smaller towns and villages, where traditions are preserved with a genuine sense of pride. For instance, the town of Nis hosts a traditional Christmas fair featuring folklore performances, artisanal crafts, and culinary delights that breathe life into the town square. Meanwhile, in Vrnjačka Banja, a popular spa town, the market scene thrives with an array of nativity scenes and carol singing events that capture the holiday spirit beautifully.

One of the most cherished customs is the preparation for the Badnje Veče, or Christmas Eve. This time focuses on family and community, as people gather to share a special meal, reflecting the spirit of unity and gratitude. It's traditional to serve a vegan feast, symbolizing purity and the anticipation of the holiday. Dishes include beans, cabbage, nuts, honey, and the star of the evening, česnica—a special bread with a coin hidden inside for luck. That sense of home, warmth, and comradery offers visitors a glimpse not just into a festive celebration, but into the heart of Serbian life.

In the countryside, riverbanks and snowy landscapes create picturesque settings for festive events. It's not unusual to encounter sleigh rides pulled by robust horses, cutting paths through snow-laden paths. The scene is straight out of a winter postcard, yet it comes alive with the laughter and excitement of families partaking in these age-old practices.

Serbia is also a place where spirituality and festivity walk hand in hand. Churches illuminate the night with candlelight processions, while the sound of bells heralding the birth of Christ resonates through valleys and across plains. Visiting a Serbian Orthodox church during this time is a spiritually uplifting experience, where the ornate iconography and holy chants transport you into a transcendent celebration of faith and humanity.

As the festivities continue, there are plenty of opportunities for more modern festivities, too. Kopaonik, Serbia's premier ski resort, entices adventure seekers with winter sports and après-ski activities, providing a mix of traditional and contemporary holiday experiences. After a day on the slopes, visitors can gather around bonfires with hot drinks while local musicians play. It's a perfect blend of rugged winter thrill and Serbian hospitality.

Serbia's vibrant holiday traditions offer something truly special—a unique combination of the old and new, rural and urban, sacred and secular. Whether you're watching the serene snowfall over historical monasteries or joining in the lively merriment of a city market, the warmth of Serbian hospitality is unwavering. It's a place where the festive season isn't just celebrated; it's lived and felt deeply, a powerful reminder of the universal joys of the holiday season.

For those eager to explore a Christmas market like no other, Serbia's vibrant traditions promise a rich and rewarding experience. It's a call to discover the heart of the Balkans amidst twinkling lights and time-honored traditions, leaving every traveler with memories that remain long after the last winter snows have melted.

Chapter 16:
The Unique Allure of Eastern Mediterranean Markets

As you wander through the vibrant tapestry of Eastern Mediterranean Christmas markets, you'll experience an enchanting fusion of history, culture, and seasonal cheer that sets them apart from their European counterparts. Picture yourself strolling through a maze of stalls in Greece and Turkey, where local artisans showcase their crafts amidst the aroma of spiced wine and roasted chestnuts. Each market exudes its own unique charm, interweaving traditional customs with the festive flair of the season, offering a sensory journey like no other. In Greece, the historic backdrop complements the festive decorations, while in Turkey, you'll discover a rich mosaic of cultural influences blending in the colorful displays. These markets don't just invite you to shop; they beckon you to explore a world where ancient traditions and holiday spirit coexist in harmonious celebration. Whether it's the sound of local music or the sight of intricate handicrafts, the Eastern Mediterranean markets promise memories wrapped in warmth and joy.

Greece's Festive Fusion

The Eastern Mediterranean, renowned for its rich tapestry of cultures and history, offers a unique setting for festive celebrations, and Greece stands out with its distinctive blend of tradition and warmth. Unlike the classic image of snow-laden Christmas markets, Greece's festive allure is bathed in the gentle glow of winter sun, reflecting both its ancient heritage and modern flair. Here, Christmas is not just a celebration; it's a time where the past and present merge, weaving together pagan traditions and Christian rituals in a captivating dance that draws locals and travelers alike.

In the heart of Athens, Syntagma Square transforms into a vibrant hub of holiday cheer. The city's renowned central landmark becomes adorned with twinkling lights and a towering Christmas tree that casts its luminous magic over bustling street stalls. These markets echo with the sounds of laughter and the tantalizing aroma of traditional treats like "melomakarona" and "kourabiedes," offering visitors a taste of sweet Greek hospitality. Shoppers stroll casually, sipping on "rakomelo," a comforting blend of raki and honey, while children glide across temporary ice-skating rinks with glee.

But the charm of Greek Christmas markets extends beyond the capital. Thessaloniki, nestled in the north, offers its own distinctive touch. The city embraces its diverse influences by incorporating local customs and gastronomic delights. Here, market stalls boast handmade crafts and aromatic spices that hint at the rich culinary history of the region. The city's waterfront promenade becomes a winter wonderland where storytellers spin mesmerizing tales of Hellenic heroes and mythical creatures, captivating audiences young and old.

Greece's festive fusion is not solely confined to the urban landscape. The picturesque islands, typically playgrounds for summer revelers, reveal a quieter, enchanting side during the winter months. Take Crete, for example, where Christmas markets spring to life with local artisans showcasing their talents. Under the watchful eye of the majestic White Mountains, visitors can discover intricately woven textiles, handcrafted leather goods, and ceramics that embody the island's artistic spirit.

The island of Rhodes, famed for its medieval charm, becomes a canvas of holiday festivities showcasing a unique fusion of Greek and Western traditions. It's common to witness carol singing parades winding through cobblestone streets, and knights in festive regalia recalling the island's storied past. Each event, accompanied by a sense of community and warmth, invites visitors to partake in a celebration that transcends time.

The essence of the Greek Christmas experience can also be found in its music. As bands play traditional tunes blended with modern rhythms, the streets resonate with the harmonious sounds of "kalanta," or Greek carols. These songs, often accompanied by simple instruments like triangles and accordions, capture the joyous spirit of the season, inviting everyone to celebrate under the starry Mediterranean sky.

What truly sets Greece apart is its continued embrace of age-old traditions that date back to antiquity. Local communities throughout the nation pay homage to the Agios Vasilis, or Saint Basil, who is celebrated on New Year's Day. Folktales once spoken by grandmothers describe his journey through the mountains of Anatolia, bringing gifts and joy. This celebration is an integral part of the Greek holiday spirit, emphasizing family unity and heartfelt generosity.

A visit to Greece's festive markets wouldn't be complete without succumbing to the culinary temptations that dot the landscape. Meander through the alleyways and you'll encounter vendors offering savory "loukoumades," delightful doughnuts drizzled with honey and sprinkled with cinnamon. The scent of roasting chestnuts fills the air, their warmth providing comfort against the crisp winter breeze. And for those seeking a more substantial meal, the traditional "souvlaki" or "spanakopita" find their rightful place amidst the festive fare.

As the winter sun sets, casting a golden hue over the whitewashed buildings and ancient ruins, there's a sense of enchantment that envelops the Greek countryside. It's not just a season; it's an experience that beckons you to see beyond the usual. Greece, with its deep-rooted traditions and welcoming spirit, invites you to join in a celebration that feels both foreign and familiar, making each visitor feel like they've arrived home.

In essence, Greece's festive fusion is an invitation to explore a magical world where time-honored customs blend seamlessly with today's modern festivities. It's a destination that offers an unforgettable experience, one that illuminates the beauty of Hellenic culture while bringing warmth and joy to the holiday season. So, whether you're wandering the ancient streets of Athens or basking in the quiet beauty of an island village, Greece promises a Christmas like no other.

Turkey's Cultural Blend

Turkey's charm in the Eastern Mediterranean is woven together like an elaborate tapestry, rich with diverse threads of history and culture. Nestled at the crossroads of Europe and Asia, Turkey offers a melting pot of influences, giving its Christmas markets a unique allure that's both exotic and familiar. While Christmas isn't traditionally celebrated in the predominantly Muslim country, urban areas, particularly Istanbul, have embraced the cosmopolitan spirit of festive markets inspired by European counterparts.

In Istanbul, the energy of the city resonates with a delightful blend of East and West. The streets come alive with strings of twinkling lights, holiday music, and the enticing aromas of roasted chestnuts mingling with the sweet scent of Turkish delight. It's a sensory feast that greets every traveler with warmth and hospitality, welcoming them into a world where ancient traditions and modern festivities coexist.

One can't overlook the grand display of Turkish crafts that these markets showcase. Artisans proudly present handwoven carpets, intricate ceramics, and ornate lamps that reflect centuries-old craftsmanship. These are more than just souvenirs; they are pieces of art that tell stories of a region steeped in history and tradition. Travelers have the unique opportunity to purchase these items directly from the craftsmen, supporting local talent and preserving an intimate piece of Turkish culture.

Diversity extends to the culinary offerings in Turkey's market scene. Stalls brim with a fusion of flavors that highlight the nation's rich gastronomic heritage. Turkish tea in delicate tulip-shaped glasses serves as the perfect companion to baklava, its sweet layers of filo pastry, nuts, and honey evoking time-honored recipes. At the same time, vendors offer more contemporary delicacies, such as chocolate-dipped fruits and globally-inspired confections, ensuring that each palate finds its delight.

Of course, the chilly air of the Turkish winter calls for something warm and aromatic. Many visitors find themselves drawn to the warm glow of the shops offering sahlep, a traditional winter beverage made from orchid root flour and milk. Dusting it with cinnamon adds a hint of spice and delight, making it a cherished drink for locals and visitors alike. It's these simple pleasures that often linger in the memory long after leaving the bustling market scene.

As footsteps echo through cobblestone streets lined with vibrant markets, the sound of music fills the air, bridging the gap between cultures. Turkish folk music harmonizes with international holiday tunes, uniting people under the shared joy of festive celebration. It's a testament to Turkey's enduring spirit of inclusion and celebration, inviting all to partake, regardless of their background or beliefs.

The architecture around these markets is as captivating as the stalls themselves. The majestic Hagia Sophia and the towering minarets of the Blue Mosque serve as stunning backdrops, reminding visitors of Turkey's significant role in bridging civilizations. These historical landmarks stand in silent testament to the myriad cultures that have passed through, each leaving a lasting impression that continues to shape Turkey's identity today.

Moreover, Turkey's cultural blend is evident in its people, who carry the traditions of their ancestors with pride while embracing the new with open arms. Engaging with locals provides a deeper understanding and appreciation of Turkish customs. Their stories offer insights into family traditions during the winter season, often revolving around food, family gatherings, and hospitality rather than gift-giving, as is common in Western celebrations.

The country's diverse geography also plays a role in the uniqueness of its festive atmosphere. From the snow-capped mountains of the east to the sunlit Izmir coastline, the seasonal variations across Turkey provide a range of experiences for those exploring its markets. Whether one is strolling through a bustling urban center or a quaint seaside town, the spirit of celebration permeates every corner, enhanced by the stunning natural beauty that surrounds.

In essence, Turkey's Christmas market scene is a testament to its ability to adapt and thrive as a cultural melting pot. It seamlessly blends old with new, tradition with innovation, and Eastern influences with Western customs. This dynamic synthesis creates a setting that is both enchanting and educational, offering travelers an exceptional glimpse into the heart of Eastern Mediterranean hospitality and culture.

For those eager to explore a different kind of Christmas spirit, Turkey's markets provide an unforgettable journey. It's a chance to experience familiar traditions in an unfamiliar setting, broadening one's perspective while embracing the shared humanity that festive celebrations naturally evoke. As Turkey continues to open its doors to the world, its cultural blend enriches every visitor, leaving a lasting impression of a country that, through its markets, unites diversity in the glow of festive warmth.

Chapter 17:
Christmas in the United States

From the iconic ice skating rink beneath the towering Christmas tree at Rockefeller Center to the vibrant displays of lights adorning the city streets, New York transforms into a winter wonderland during the holiday season, with its markets offering a sensory feast of aromas, sights, and festive sounds. The annual Union Square Holiday Market is a testament to the city's multicultural spirit, presenting an array of handcrafted goods, tantalizing food stalls, and unique gifts that reflect the diverse and dynamic culture of the Big Apple. Meanwhile, Chicago embraces the spirit of the season with its own festive charm, notably at the Christkindlmarket in Daley Plaza, where the enchantment of a traditional German market comes alive in the heart of the Windy City. Amidst the wooden booths and twinkling lights, visitors can savor Bavarian pretzels, explore handcrafted toys, and immerse themselves in the joyous atmosphere that draws inspiration from deep-rooted European traditions while proudly celebrating local flavor. These bustling markets not only capture the joy and warmth of the holiday season but also underscore the unique melting pot of traditions and cultures that come together to create an unforgettable American Christmas experience.

New York's Iconic Markets

As the holiday season descends upon New York City, the already bustling metropolis transforms into a magical wonderland. The city, vibrant and eclectic, celebrates Christmas with a series of festive markets that reflect its diverse cultural tapestry. These iconic markets offer not just a chance to shop but an opportunity to immerse oneself in the warmth, nostalgia, and spectacle that defines a New York Christmas.

The most famous of these markets is undoubtedly the Union Square Holiday Market. Nestled in the heart of Manhattan, this market hosts over a hundred vendors, each offering unique gifts and artisanal crafts. The market's strategic location and reputation make it a magnet for both New Yorkers and visitors. Walking through the labyrinth of stalls, the smell of warm pretzels and hot chocolate fills the air, weaving an aromatic tapestry that captures the essence of the season.

Next, don't miss out on exploring the holiday market at Bryant Park, officially known as the Winter Village. This market, surrounded by the towering skyscrapers of Midtown, creates a striking visual contrast that is unmistakably New York. The village comes alive with twinkling lights, shimmering decorations, and the gentle hum of laughter and conversation. Vendors, sourced from local artisans and small business owners, present an array of handcrafted goods ranging from delicate jewelry to vibrant artwork. At the center lies the skating rink, where visitors can glide beneath the stars, completing the picturesque setting.

Grand Central Terminal's Holiday Fair presents another iconic New York experience. Unlike the outdoor markets, Grand Central offers a cozy indoor retreat from the brisk winter air. Here, under the magnificent ceiling of the historic terminal, shoppers can explore a curated selection of high-quality crafts and gifts. The hustle of commuters, combined with the festive energy of the fair, creates a dynamic backdrop that embodies the city's spirit. It's an experience that seamlessly marries New York's industrious character with the joyous essence of Christmas.

For a taste of authentic European-style festivities, the German Christmas Market at Central Park's Columbus Circle echoes the traditional markets of Nuremberg and Munich. Visitors are drawn to its warm glow, the stalls adorned with greenery and soft lights. Amidst the array of German delicacies, like bratwurst and gingerbread, the market offers crafts and ornaments that evoke European charm and traditional craftsmanship. The market is not only a place to shop but a bridge to experiencing cultures through sweets, stories, and shared smiles.

While each market offers its unique atmosphere and attractions, they collectively celebrate the universal joy of the holiday season. Wandering through these markets, one can find that perfect gift or stumble upon a delightful culinary treat hidden amidst the hustle. The sense of community is palpable as families, tourists, and locals come together, sharing in the simple pleasures of the season.

These markets are more than just shopping destinations; they're living stories of New York's spirit and diversity. Amidst the whirl of carolers, the tinkling laughter of children, and the crisp rustle of shoppers shuffling by, they create a sense of warmth and inclusiveness. Each market is a microcosm of the city itself—a place where tradition meets modernity, where every visitor becomes part of the larger tapestry.

New York's iconic markets remind us that the magic of Christmas is not confined to any one place or tradition. They invite us to pause, to savor the richness of different cultures, and to celebrate the art of giving. These markets are emblematic of a season where the simple joys of life are brought to the forefront, renewed each year with a dazzling array of color, light, and sound.

So, as you stroll through New York's holiday markets, take a moment to appreciate not just the shopping, but the shared humanity. In each smile exchanged, in every warm cup of cider, and through simple acts of kindness, the essence of Christmas and the spirit of New York intertwine, creating memories that linger well beyond the season. The gleaming markets under New York's winter sky become, in this way, more than festivity—they're an invitation to experience the boundless joy that this wonderful city holds.

Chicago's Festive Diversity

In the heart of the Midwest, where the chill of winter sets the stage for holiday magic, Chicago emerges as a kaleidoscope of festive diversity. This vibrant city, celebrated for its architectural prowess and rich cultural tapestry, transforms into a winter wonderland as Christmas approaches. The Magnificent Mile glistens with twinkling lights, an enticing prelude to the treasures that await throughout the city's neighborhoods.

Chicago's Christkindlmarket, inspired by Germany's famed holiday markets, serves as the city's crown jewel of Christmas festivities. Set against the backdrop of downtown skyscrapers in Daley Plaza, this market is a sensory delight. The aroma of spiced mulled wine, or *Glühwein*, invites visitors to explore the wooden stalls that brim with handcrafted ornaments, intricate cuckoo clocks, and artisanal goods. Vendors, hailing both from local communities and distant lands, offer an array of crafts that echo their cultural origins. Here, traditions are not just preserved but celebrated, creating a melting pot of Christmas cheer.

Yet, Chicago's festive spirit doesn't stop at the bustling aisles of Christkindlmarket. Millennium Park is another focal point of holiday joy, where the iconic Cloud Gate sculpture is gracefully enveloped by snow and lights. The ice-skating rink that flanks the park is a scene of joyous activity, where families and couples spin and glide beneath the city skyline. Nearby, the annual holiday lights ceremony at the park draws crowds eager to partake in music, light shows, and the tree-lighting event, marking the official start to the holiday season.

Chicago's neighborhoods, each a vibrant homage to the city's multicultural identity, offer their own unique takes on holiday celebrations. In the historically European enclave of Polish and Eastern European communities, Christmas traditions are celebrated with fervor and authenticity. Polish neighborhoods like Avondale and Jefferson Park are adorned with *łapki*—ornamental wheat sheaves accented with ribbons—while community churches host traditional Masses characterized by solemnity and sweet carols.

Head south to Pilsen, and you're met with bright displays of Mexican *Navidad* traditions. Luminarias light up the streets in honor of Las Posadas, narrating the biblical journey of Mary and Joseph. In these bustling streets, street vendors serve warm tamales and steaming cups of *atole*, a sweet cornmeal drink. This culinary fare, paired with the rhythmic sounds of *mariachi* bands, paints a vibrant scene of cultural fusion and holiday delight.

Not far from Pilsen, the neighborhood of Bronzeville offers a different rhythm as it celebrates Kwanzaa, honoring African-American heritage and cultural identity. Community centers host workshops and event series that promote unity and creativity, attracting both residents and visitors. At the heart of these celebrations lies an emphasis on community, creativity, and reflection, infused with a festive spirit that complements the broader holiday atmosphere of the city.

Little Italy presents its own blend of Christmas traditions, with authentic Italian feasts and a strong religious presence in the community. The Feast of the Seven Fishes, an Italian-American tradition, features prominently on Christmas Eve, as families gather over sumptuous seafood meals that speak to the rich maritime heritage of their forebears. Churches in the area radiate with solemn liturgical celebrations, wreathing the local streets and businesses in festive reverence.

As one ventures into the neighborhoods of Andersonville and Uptown, you're greeted with the distinct flavors of Swedish and Vietnamese holiday influences. Andersonville, with its deep Swedish roots, shines bright with *Julbord* feasts and the dulcet glow of candelabras on windowsills. Meanwhile, Uptown is a patchwork of Vietnamese festivities that harmoniously blend Christmas and the Buddhist celebration of Tết, creating a unique holiday mosaic where tradition meets innovation.

Throughout the city, public art installations, crafted by local artists, play a role in connecting the diverse festive themes. Displays pay homage to Chicago's cultural history and offer the world a glimpse into the narrative of this awe-inspiring city during the holidays. Art becomes a living thing here, an extension of the celebrations, capturing the hearts of onlookers and inciting a sense of unity—a hallmark of Chicago's festive season.

There's a lasting warmth amid the brisk winds of Lake Michigan during the holiday season in Chicago. Whether it's the shared laughter over a steaming cup of hot chocolate, the communal gathering to witness a light parade, or the simple joy of viewing holiday window displays on State Street, the city steals everyone's hearts during this special time of year. It's a place where diverse traditions blend seamlessly; a place where every corner of the city tells a different yet beautifully interconnected festive story.

Chapter 18: Canada's Winter Marvels

Canada transforms into a winter wonderland during the festive season, offering enchanting experiences that make it a must-see destination for Christmas market enthusiasts. Amidst the crisp, chilly air and the serene blanket of snow, Canada's markets are alive with vibrant colors, jubilant sounds, and the tantalizing aroma of seasonal treats. In Montreal, the joyful festivities draw locals and tourists alike to streets lined with stalls brimming with handcrafted gifts and gourmet delights, fostering a warm community spirit against the backdrop of historic architecture. Meanwhile, Toronto dazzles with its spectacular display of holiday lights, where each corner of the city sparkles with festive cheer, offering visitors endless photo opportunities and the chance to experience local customs and cuisine. Both cities encapsulate the magic of a Canadian Christmas, blending traditional celebrations with cultural diversity, making them destinations where the heart of winter shines bright, warming every soul that ventures into their festive embrace.

Montreal's Joyful Festivities

Among Canada's winter marvels, Montreal stands out as a beacon of festive joy, offering enchanting experiences that captivate both locals and visitors alike. As the first snowflakes begin to dust the city's vibrant streets, Montreal transforms into a holiday haven. Wandering through the city's cobblestone streets feels like stepping into a snow globe, where the warmth of the festivities balances the crisp winter air.

Perched on the banks of the St. Lawrence River, Montreal boasts a blend of European charm and North American style that makes its Christmas markets truly unique. The city is a tapestry of cultures, and this diversity is vividly displayed throughout the holiday season. From mid-November to the end of December, the city's markets are alive with twinkling lights, festive music, and the irresistible aroma of holiday treats.

Atwater Market is a bustling hub that draws visitors with its spectacular display of lights and decorations. As you stroll through the market, you can spot vendors offering an array of handcrafted goods that are perfect for that one-of-a-kind holiday gift. The echo of carolers' harmonious songs intertwines with the laughter of children marveling at the whimsical holiday installations.

Not far off, the Jean-Talon Market offers another cozy corner where the spirit of the season thrives. Known for its fresh local produce and artisanal products, the market becomes a winter wonderland that lures visitors with hot cocoa, mulled wine, and sweet delights. Vendors offer everything from handmade ornaments to delicious Quebecois specialties like tourtière and maple taffy. It's a mélange of tastes and sights that embody the city's vibrant spirit.

The Great Montreal Outdoor Christmas Market takes center stage in downtown, where the scent of roasted chestnuts mingles with the brisk winter air. This market is where Montreal's diverse cultural tapestry truly shines. Stalls brim with goods from around the world, reflecting the city's multicultural soul. You can find unique crafts alongside culinary adventures like poutine topped with foie gras, a twist on traditional favorites that celebrates Montreal's culinary creativity.

Winter Wonderlands

A highlight of Montreal's festive scene is the Place des Festivals, where interactive lights and art installations create an immersive experience that enchants visitors of all ages. This is a place where technology and tradition meet, forming a modern landscape that still feels timeless. At night, fireworks light up the sky, mirroring the city below it, celebrating the joyful spirit that defines this season.

A centerpiece of the city's holiday celebrations is the Montreal Christmas Village set against the iconic Notre-Dame Basilica. This quaint market lures with its picturesque stalls and charming variety of handmade goods. Here, the air is filled with cheerful greetings as people explore the rows of vendors offering lovingly crafted gifts and gourmet treats. The basilica's festive backdrop adds a magical element, enhancing the village's old-world charm.

The heart of Montreal's holiday cheer beats strong in its communal events. Parades wind through downtown streets, where families gather to witness vibrant floats and marching bands spreading festive cheer. Local artists often perform, adding a soundtrack of joy to the already lively atmosphere.

Montrealers are known for their love of the outdoors, even as temperatures drop. This spirit is captured in the city's free-spirited approach to enjoying the season. Ice skating rinks dot the city, offering locals and tourists the chance to glide joyously amidst the twinkling lights. The Old Port's Natrel Skating Rink features stunning views of the historic district, making it a popular spot for those seeking a different kind of winter wonder.

For a true taste of Montreal's cultural diversity, visitors can attend the annual Festival Noël dans le Parc. This event is a unique blend of outdoor concerts, plays, and creative workshops set against the backdrop of picturesque urban parks sprinkled with holiday cheer. Performances from local musicians and storytellers bring a laid-back vibe, inviting guests to stay warm around bonfires, sipping on homemade cider as they soak in the communal warmth.

Montreal's holiday season represents more than just a celebration; it's a testament to the city's ability to meld its rich history with modern vibrancy. The city invites everyone to partake in the festivities, to leave with memories that capture the essence of what makes this city a winter marvel. So, if you find yourself in Montreal during the holiday season, prepare for a journey infused with joy, culture, and a festive spirit that warms even the coldest of days. The city embodies a joyous symphony that resonates through its markets, parades, and the shared experiences of celebration, offering an invitation that's impossible to resist.

Toronto's Holiday Lights

Toronto's holiday season transforms the cityscape into a vibrant spectacle of dazzling lights and festive cheer. A sprawling metropolis known for its multicultural vibrancy, Toronto embraces the holiday spirit with a breathtaking amalgamation of lights and celebrations that captivate locals and visitors alike. Wandering through the city during this magical time feels like stepping into a winter wonderland, with every corner offering a unique display of holiday luminosity.

The Distillery District is one of the most iconic spots to experience Toronto's holiday magic. This historic neighborhood, with its cobblestone streets and Victorian-era architecture, becomes a radiant backdrop for the Toronto Christmas Market. Dotted with twinkling lights and festive stalls, the market offers handcrafted gifts, delicious treats, and warm beverages that offer a respite from the chilly winter air. The massive Christmas tree at the heart of the market acts as a beacon, drawing the awe of visitors with its countless shimmering lights.

Winter Wonderlands

Beyond the traditional market setting, Toronto's City Hall and Nathan Phillips Square are equally mesmerizing. Here, the annual Cavalcade of Lights inaugurates the holiday season in late November. With the city's skyline as a backdrop, the event delights crowds with an impressive fireworks show and the official illumination of Toronto's towering Christmas tree. Ice-skaters glide gracefully on the outdoor rink, bathed in the glow of thousands of LED lights that decorate the surrounding trees and structures.

Elsewhere in the city, one can find a cacophony of cultures blending harmoniously in the celebration of the holidays. Neighborhoods like Little Italy, Greektown, and Chinatown dress their streets in festive attire, reflecting their unique traditions and adds a distinctive touch to Toronto's holiday tableau. During this time, storefronts compete for the most elaborate displays, while street performers and carolers fill the air with joyful sounds.

For those seeking a more intimate encounter with Toronto's holiday lights, the Toronto Islands provide an enchanting escape. A short ferry ride offers a sweeping view of the city's skyline, twinkling with festive lights. The islands become a serene backdrop for winter activities like snowshoeing and cross-country skiing, with the distant twinkle of the city's lights ever visible across the lake.

In recent years, neighborhoods throughout Toronto have embraced the spirit of competition with elaborate home light displays. Beaconsfield Village, famously known for its mesmerizing decorations, sees community members rally together to outshine one another with creative and colorful displays, drawing crowds from all over the Greater Toronto Area.

The Art Gallery of Ontario and the Royal Ontario Museum also contribute to the seasonal festivities, offering special holiday exhibitions and programs. Families and art enthusiasts gather here, finding warmth in shared cultural experiences and discovering the joy of seeing galleries come to life through the lens of holiday cheer.

Toronto's festive magic isn't confined to the downtown core. Head towards Scarborough, and the Toronto Zoo offers another luminous spectacle with its annual "Terra Lumina" experience. This immersive walk-through adventure seamlessly blends storytelling with light installations, casting a magical glow over the zoo's winter landscape, while hinting at messages of conservation and hope for the future.

In the heart of downtown, the Eaton Centre attracts visitors with its seasonal transformation. One of the tallest indoor Christmas trees in Canada stands here, adorned with dazzling ornaments that draw holiday shoppers and sightseers. As you wander through this retail haven, the festive atmosphere is palpable, enhanced by musical performances and decorative installations.

For those yearning for a theatrical experience, Toronto's entertainment district offers a myriad of holiday-themed performances. The National Ballet of Canada traditionally enchants audiences with its rendition of 'The Nutcracker', while theaters around the city present everything from classic Christmas plays to contemporary shows that capture the festive spirit.

While much of Toronto's holiday sparkle is visual, the sensory experience extends to taste and smell. The city's diverse range of culinary offerings ensures that every outing comes with the possibility of savoring holiday treats, from traditional mince pies to poutines with a seasonal twist. Food festivals and pop-up events highlight everything from the latest in food trends to classic holiday flavors, ensuring every palate is satisfied.

In a city marked by its multicultural tapestry, Toronto's Holiday Lights serve not merely as decoration but as symbols of unity and celebration. Each bulb, each twinkle, adds to the collective narrative of a city that warmly embraces both the cold winter and the festive season. The lights bring people together, transcending generations and backgrounds, encouraging everyone to come together to share in the city's jubilant energy.

Toronto's holiday illuminations captivate the hearts of many, creating lasting memories and becoming an annual tradition for countless families. As the season rolls around each year, residents and visitors alike look forward to the lights not just for their beauty but for the sense of community, warmth, and joy they inspire in the midst of Toronto's snowy streets.

Chapter 19:
South America's Holiday Celebrations

In South America, the holiday season bursts into life with a vibrant celebration of cultural diversity and tropical flair. While snowflakes and chilly breezes may define Christmas elsewhere, here, it's the warmth of the sun and the spirit of community that sets the festive mood. Brazil's lively festivities, filled with music, dance, and colorful parades, are a reflection of its rich cultural tapestry, blending African, European, and indigenous influences. From the bustling streets of Rio de Janeiro to the serene and picturesque settings in smaller towns, the celebrations are marked by a unique blend of tradition and modernity. Meanwhile, in Argentina, the holiday season is a harmonious mix of European customs and local flavors. Families gather to share asados and enjoy fireworks, and the vibrant markets come alive with artisan crafts and tango melodies. It's a time when the joy of the season envelops towns and cities, creating a unifying bond among people from all walks of life. As South America embraces the holidays, visitors find themselves swept up in the warmth and jubilance, making memories in a land where tradition and festivity meet the summer sun.

Brazil's Tropical Traditions

When one dreams of holiday celebrations, visions of snow-dusted pine trees, steaming mugs of hot cocoa, and markets bustling with gloved shoppers might come to mind. Yet, Brazil offers a compelling contrast with its vibrant and tropical twist on Christmas festivities. Here, the yuletide season is bathed not in the glow of candlelight reflecting off snow but in the sun's warm embrace and the dynamic rhythms echoing through its streets. Revelers across the country embrace this festive period with open-air events that overflow with music, dance, and the unmistakable aroma of traditional foods.

Brazilians celebrate Christmas, or "Natal," in a manner that's as diverse as the country itself, blending religious traditions with joyous public celebrations. Given its deep-rooted Catholic heritage, many of Brazil's holiday rituals revolve around the nativity story and significant religious ceremonies. Midnight Mass, known as "Missa do Galo," is held on Christmas Eve and draws large crowds to the country's beautiful churches, which are often expertly decorated with lights and nativity scenes.

In true Brazilian fashion, religion goes hand in hand with celebration. Known for their love of music and dance, it's no surprise that holiday cheer spills onto the streets in a series of vibrant parades and festivals. In cities like Rio de Janeiro and São Paulo, the celebrations are marked by grandiose fireworks displays that light up the sky, bringing communities together in festive harmony. These events highlight the country's knack for blending solemnity with spirited celebration.

Brazilian Christmas markets, while not as traditional as their European counterparts, have started to gain popularity, offering a rich tapestry of local artisanship and flavors. Craft vendors sell handmade ornaments, jewelry, and an array of gifts that capture Brazil's unique culture and spirit. Shoppers meander through stalls that are adorned with colorful decorations, enveloping themselves in the lively melodies of samba and bossa nova, which provide a distinctly tropical soundtrack to the season's festivities.

Food plays a central role in Brazil's holiday traditions, with families gathering to feast upon an abundance of dishes that blend native ingredients with global influences. The Christmas meal is often a potluck of sorts, featuring turkey, ham, and freshly caught fish items like the Brazilian delicacy, bacalhau (salted cod). Farofa, a toasted cassava flour mixture, often accompanies the meal, adding a hearty, satisfying crunch. Desserts are equally important, with rabanada, Brazil's version of French toast, and pudim, a rich caramel flan, adding sweetness to the holiday menu.

Despite the absence of snow, many Brazilians enjoy creating "Papai Noel" or Santa Claus displays, often incorporating imaginative tropical variations. It's not unusual to see "Santa" arriving on a surfboard or dressed in lighter, more climate-appropriate clothing, replacing his traditional attire. These whimsical interpretations add a unique Brazilian flair to the season, delighting children and adults alike with their playful creativity.

The tradition of the "amigo secreto," or secret friend, also finds its way into Brazilian holiday gatherings, much like the Western Secret Santa. Friends, families, and coworkers exchange gifts anonymously, fostering a sense of community and surprise that perfectly complements the pleasures of the festive season. While the names are drawn and gifts are exchanged, laughter and camaraderie fill the air, further strengthening the bonds of friendship and family.

Brazil's coastal cities, especially places such as Florianópolis and Salvador, add a beachside twist to the holiday spirit, offering sun-drenched sands and ocean breezes to those who live or vacation there. Many take to the beaches on Christmas Day for barbecues and picnics, enjoying grilled seafood and fresh tropical fruit under the shade of swaying palm trees. It's a relaxed and joyful ambiance that embodies the laid-back and genial Brazilian way of life.

Festivities continue right past Christmas with the revelry of New Year's Eve, a time when Brazilians light fireworks and partake in traditional rituals meant to usher in good fortune for the coming year.

In cities such as Rio, the famed Copacabana beach fills with people wearing white, a symbol of peace and renewal. As the clock strikes midnight, this sea of white turns into a jubilant dance party under the stars, a brilliant culmination that seamlessly links into the vibrancy of the impending Carnival season.

In Brazil, Christmas isn't just a day—it's an unfolding celebration melding time-honored practices with modern expressions of joy. It's a testament to how traditions adapt and thrive in new climates, reflecting the diversity and warmth of the Brazilian people. From its bustling cities to its quiet rural landscapes, Brazil's tropical traditions showcase a country where the spirit of togetherness and festivity finds new, captivating ways to touch hearts during the holiday season.

The charm of Brazil's tropical Christmas is inimitable. It's a reminder of how celebrations can transcend the traditional imagery of a winter wonderland, evoking a reassurance that holiday spirit can be found anywhere in the world. As one takes in the sights and sounds of Brazil during the Christmas period, there is a profound sense of inclusiveness, welcoming any who wish to partake in this extraordinary celebration of life, light, and love.

Argentina's Festive Blend

Amid the vibrant tapestry of South America, Argentina stands out with its unique blend of Christmas traditions, woven from the threads of its rich cultural and historical heritage. Unlike the snowy scenes associated with the holidays in the Northern Hemisphere, Argentina's festive season is draped in summer warmth, bringing a distinct and lively twist to celebrations. The streets buzz with the energy of long summer days, inviting locals and visitors alike to explore a festive dimension that's unmistakably Argentine.

At the heart of Argentina's Christmas charm is the spirit of togetherness and familial bonds. The festive season is a time when families gather, often traveling from different corners of the country to reunite in their hometowns or the bustling capital, Buenos Aires. The celebrations kick off on Christmas Eve, or "Nochebuena," with a sumptuous feast that starts late in the evening and extends into the early hours of Christmas Day. Tables brim with traditional delicacies like "asado," the quintessential Argentine barbecue, and a variety of salads and cold dishes perfect for the summer heat. Everyone shares a toast with a flute of sparkling wine or cider as the clock strikes midnight, marking the moment with fireworks lighting up the sky and filling the air with a festive crescendo.

The nativity scene or "pesebre" is a prominent feature in Argentine homes during the holiday season. It's more than just a decorative piece; crafting the nativity scene is a cherished tradition that involves the entire family. The scenes vary in complexity and size, often becoming a centerpiece for storytelling and reflection on the origins of Christmas. While some families opt for simple setups, others go all out, incorporating intricate details and even small figurines that represent local fauna, adding a touch of Argentine flair to a universal scene.

In Buenos Aires, the holiday spirit is best captured through the city's vibrant parades and festivals. The parade in Plaza de Mayo is a highlight, drawing crowds with its lively processions, colorful costumes, and the joyful sounds of street musicians. As the city dresses itself in holiday lights, walking through neighborhoods like Palermo and Recoleta becomes an enchanting experience. Each storefront and tree seems infused with magic, enhancing the festive ambiance.

One can't miss the "Feria Navideña" or Christmas market, which pops up in various parts of Buenos Aires. These markets offer a delightful blend of traditional Argentine crafts and imported holiday goods. Wander through the stalls, and you'll find handcrafted ornaments, vibrant textiles, and whimsical toys for children. Local artisans display their talents, creating unique pieces that reflect the diverse influences of Argentina's cultural mosaic. Food stalls tempt visitors with empanadas, churros, and sweet treats like "panettone," showcasing the country's culinary fusion influenced by its Italian heritage.

Mendoza, nestled at the foot of the Andes, is another city where Christmas takes on a unique identity. Known for its vineyards and outstanding wines, the holiday season in Mendoza is a time when wine tasting becomes a festive activity, drawing both locals and tourists. Wineries open their doors, offering visitors a chance to enjoy the finest Malbec while soaking up the scenic splendor of sprawling vineyards under a sun-drenched sky. It's a perfect pairing, where the richness of Argentine wine complements the spirit of the season.

In the rural regions of Argentina, Christmas retains a more traditional and serene air. These areas often celebrate with community gatherings where caroling, or "villancicos," fills the air with joyful melodies. These gatherings are characterized by their simplicity and warmth, reflecting a pace that allows for genuine human connection. In these settings, time-honored customs like "Misa de Gallo," the midnight mass, hold significant importance, drawing communities together to reflect and rejoice in the spiritual essence of the holiday.

The influence of Spanish and Italian immigrants is palpable in Argentina's festive customs, especially in how the holiday palette includes the best of both worlds. From the Spanish tradition of setting off fireworks to the Italian-inspired panettone that's become synonymous with Christmas desserts, Argentina has skillfully cultivated a festive identity that's both borrowed and uniquely its own. This cultural intertwining enriches the holiday experience, offering those who partake a chance to witness a symphony of traditions in harmony.

New Year's Eve, or "Año Nuevo," flows seamlessly from Christmas celebrations, keeping the festive momentum going as families gather once again to welcome a new year. Dinner around this time mirrors that of Christmas Eve with elaborate spreads, signaling abundance and the promise of new beginnings. At the stroke of midnight, tradition dictates eating 12 grapes — one for each chime of the clock — symbolizing hope and luck for the year to come. Once again, the skies are set alight by fireworks, ensuring that the new year is met with joy and splendor.

Argentina's festive blend is more than a seasonal affair; it's an invitation to experience a culture deeply rooted in the joy of togetherness and vibrant life. For the travel enthusiast looking for a unique Christmas celebration, Argentina offers a heartwarming alternative to snow-laden festivities. It reminds us that the holiday spirit transcends climate and geography, taking on diverse forms that reflect the locales in which it thrives. It's a vivid mosaic of tradition and modernity, ready to welcome all those who seek to explore its joyous festivities.

Chapter 20: Asia's Festive Fusion

As the holiday season sweeps across Asia, a dazzling tapestry of traditions and modernity emerges, captivating travelers with its vibrant allure. In Japan, the streets come alive with mesmerizing light displays that transform cityscapes into enchanting wonderlands, where the concept of illumination reaches new artistic heights. Meanwhile, South Korea bursts with festive energy, as its cities host grand holiday extravaganzas blending cultural festivities with contemporary flair. Here, Christmas markets brim with unique culinary delights, enticing aromas of roasting chestnuts, and the soft glow of lanterns, offering travelers a sensory experience like no other. These celebrations mirror Asia's unique ability to harmonize age-old customs with innovative flair, creating an unforgettable festive fusion that warmly beckons holiday enthusiasts from around the globe. Whether you're strolling through illuminated pathways or exploring vibrant markets, Asia's celebrations promise an unforgettable journey into the heart of holiday wonder.

Japan's Illuminated Celebrations

Japan offers a beguiling array of illuminated celebrations that capture both the traditional spirit and the innovative flair of this fascinating nation. As the year winds down, major cities across Japan sparkle with a dazzling display of lights, setting the stage for holiday festivities that draw locals and tourists alike. Here, Christmas is more about a visual feast than a religious ritual, offering a unique way to embrace the holiday spirit.

At the heart of Japan's illuminated revelry is the brilliant display of lights or "illuminations" as they're commonly known. Travelers to cities like Tokyo, Kyoto, and Osaka will find themselves enveloped in a sea of glowing displays that transform individual cityscapes into realms of fantasy. These annual events have become a beloved tradition, eagerly anticipated for the joy and wonder they ignite in the hearts of people from all walks of life.

In Tokyo, the Marunouchi area boasts one of the longest-running illumination shows. Thousands flock to the prestigious district to witness the nearly one million energy-efficient LED bulbs bringing the trees along the streets to life. Meanwhile, the vibrant shopping district of Shibuya, known for its high-energy vibe, curates its own scintillating light displays. Scrambling through the famous Shibuya crossing, the pulsating lights blend with the modern metropolis, inducing a festive yet futuristic atmosphere.

Joining the pageant of lights is none other than the Tokyo Midtown complex in Roppongi. Each year, the Starlight Garden springs to life with its breathtaking portrayal of constellations, creating a celestial experience that marries the earthly wonders of technology with the ethereal beauty of the universe. It's like walking through a galaxy of shimmering stars, all set within the capital's urban core.

Head westward to the traditional city of Kyoto, where lights take on an atmospheric elegance that aligns with the city's historical heritage. Arashiyama's famed Bamboo Grove is often transformed into a magical walkway, where the bamboo shoots themselves become part of the dazzling spectacle. This blend of nature and illumination creates an otherworldly scene that evokes Kyoto's timeless beauty while offering a captivating nod to the modern holiday season.

Winter Wonderlands

Osaka, on the other hand, delivers a different flair. Known for its lively culture and culinary delights, the city's Nakanoshima area hosts the Osaka Festival of Lights. Here, you can find the Osaka Hikari-Renaissance, a stunning display of colored lights set against the backdrop of the city's heritage buildings. Combining creativity with historical preservation, the festival captures Osaka's unique blend of progress and tradition.

Let's not forget about Sapporo, where the snow-covered landscape stops one in their tracks with its own unique beauty. The Sapporo White Illumination is nothing short of magical, turning the snow-laden trees and buildings into a fairy-tale setting that warms the heart, despite the frosty temperatures. It's the ideal location for those who revel in winter's chill, wrapped in the gentle glow of countless twinkling lights.

Japan's focus on light isn't just an urban spectacle. Moving away from the bustling cities, you'll find smaller, more intimate displays that radiate charm and warmth. These are often found in local parks and smaller towns, where community spirit shines as brightly as the illuminations themselves. They offer a serene retreat from the city crowd, enabling visitors to experience the holiday magic in a more personal, tranquil setting.

Adorning the colorful streets and unforgettable experiences, the country's famous food scene becomes an irresistible accompaniment to the visual feast. Japanese confectioneries and holiday treats are a sensory delight that adds another layer to the celebrations. Look out for unique holiday-themed eats, from dazzling cakes in department stores to piping hot bowls of ramen on street corners—a delightful fusion of global holiday tradition and local gastronomy.

Beyond the lights and treats, Japan's holidays are marked by a spirit of harmony and togetherness. Families, friends, and even colleagues come together to marvel at the illuminations, sharing in the joy and warmth that radiates through the sparkling displays. This shared experience often leaves an indelible mark on visitors, who find themselves drawn to Japan's sense of community during the festive season.

For the travel enthusiast seeking a unique and unforgettable holiday experience, Japan's illuminated celebrations offer a journey of wonder. With each twist and turn unveiling a dazzling display of creativity and cultural warmth, it's a destination that seamlessly blends tradition with modernity and invites travelers to find joy in the glow of lights and the festive spirit of togetherness.

South Korea's Holiday Extravaganza

As you step into the bustling streets of Seoul during the holiday season, you're greeted with a harmonious blend of tradition and modernity. South Korea may not be the first place that comes to mind when thinking about Christmas markets, yet its unique take on the festive season is nothing short of a holiday extravaganza. Here, the vibrancy of city life meets the warmth of traditional celebrations, offering a colorful medley that delights both locals and visitors alike.

Christmas in South Korea is more than just a religious occasion; it's a celebration of togetherness and joy that transcends boundaries. In the capital, Seoul, the holiday season is marked by stunning light displays and bustling markets that pop up throughout the city. One of the most iconic markets is located in the heart of Myeongdong. The area transforms into a winter wonderland every December, with stalls offering everything from street food favorites like tteokbokki and hotteok to Christmas-themed trinkets and gifts.

The Seoul Christmas Festival, hosted at the Cheonggyecheon Stream, is another standout event. Its picturesque setting, with a glittering stream illuminated by a symphony of lights, provides a fairy-tale backdrop for a night out with family and friends. Stretching over several kilometers, the festival incorporates a series of art installations, seasonal decorations, and live performances that make each visit a memorable experience. The charm of the Cheonggyecheon is heightened during the holidays, where one can stroll along the lit pathways, enjoying everything from choir performances to pop-up cafes serving warm treats.

Of course, the holiday season in South Korea isn't complete without mentioning Dongdaemun Design Plaza's winter market. Architecturally futuristic, this space becomes a hub of creativity and holiday cheer. From unique crafts to eye-catching installations, the market here promises a feast for the senses. Vendors offer innovative holiday merchandise, including handcrafted ornaments and bespoke gifts—perfect mementoes for travelers looking to take a piece of Korea home.

If you're yearning for a more traditional experience, head over to the lively streets of Insadong. Here, the old and new blend seamlessly, and during the holiday season, it's no different. Insadong offers a peek into the country's rich cultural tapestry, with market stalls that showcase traditional Korean arts and crafts. You can find everything from beautifully crafted Hanji (traditional Korean paper) to handmade pottery—ideal as gifts or as personal keepsakes. This area is quintessentially Korean, exuding warmth and an intimate local charm, yet with a Christmas twist.

In addition to the immersive city experiences, South Korea offers picturesque settings beyond the urban sprawl. While Seoul is a major draw, visiting Busan during this season offers its own unique charm. Busan's Jagalchi Market transforms into a festive hotspot, where dazzling lights reflect off the coastal waters creating a dreamy atmosphere. The Christmas Tree Festival in Nampo-dong is another can't-miss event. The towering tree illuminated against the night sky and the surrounding streets filled with celebratory music and laughter offer picture-perfect moments that define Yuletide cheer.

For those inclined towards icy adventures, ice skating rinks pop up in various locations. Seoul's City Hall Plaza and Olympic Park both offer impressive rinks where you can glide under twinkling lights, often to the sounds of contemporary Korean pop or festive classics. Wrapping up the day with hot cocoa from a nearby stall, while basking in the crisp winter air, epitomizes the Seoul winter experience.

Meanwhile, cinema lovers might find solace in South Korea's unique Christmas cine-culture. Many theaters, especially in major cities, host holiday-themed movie marathons, showcasing both local films and international Christmas classics. It's a beloved tradition that ends up uniting diverse audiences through the simple yet profound joy of storytelling.

Adding another layer to the experience is the culinary delights of the season. South Korea takes festive dining to new heights with a fusion of traditional Korean flavors and Western holiday cuisine. Many restaurants and cafes introduce special holiday menus, featuring popular dishes such as galbi (grilled ribs) and bulgogi (marinated beef) alongside traditional Christmas fare like roast turkey and mince pies.

While bustling marketplaces and grand light displays capture the spirit of festivities, the warmth of traditional Korean hospitality remains at the heart of South Korea's holiday marvel. The festive spirit is equally palpable in the country's picturesque villages, where ancient customs meet modern celebrations. Temples, often considered spiritual sanctuaries, host special events and offer serene settings for reflection amidst the holiday hustle. Here, visitors can partake in tea ceremonies and make traditional crafts, capturing the essence of Korean culture and the timeless beauty of a winter holiday.

In essence, South Korea's holiday extravaganza is a unique mosaic of lights, culture, and community. It invites travelers not just to witness its marvels but to immerse in a celebration that transcends cultures, merging global festivities with Korean authenticity. Each market, festival, and celebration offers a unique experience, guaranteed to leave an indelible imprint on the hearts of those who journey into this winter wonderland. Whether you find joy amidst the shimmering lights of Seoul or the coastal allure of Busan, South Korea's festive spirit is a testament to the country's enduring warmth and creativity. So why not embrace the unexpected and let South Korea surprise you with its own rendition of holiday magic?

Chapter 21:
Australia's Sunny Yuletide

Australia offers a distinctive take on the holiday season, where Christmas markets thrive under the warm sun, making it a unique destination for festive enthusiasts. Rather than the typical snowy scenes often associated with Yuletide, Australia's version combines the best of summer fun with holiday traditions. In Sydney, the vibrant markets burst with local crafts, gourmet foods, and lively performances, all reminiscent of the city's eclectic spirit. Visitors can indulge in outdoor barbecues and seafood spreads, capturing the essence of a sun-drenched Christmas. Meanwhile, Melbourne's festive traditions bring a harmonious blend of art and celebration, with open-air theaters and bustling night markets illuminating the city's diverse culture. The joyous atmosphere is contagious, and the community spirit is on full display, inviting travelers to experience a Christmas unlike any other. With a backdrop of sandy beaches and sunny skies, Australia's Yuletide presents an inspiring twist on tradition, merging the warmth of summer with the joyous spirit of the holidays.

Sydney's Unique Celebrations

Sydney, a city where the sun kisses the ocean and the vibrancy of life permeates every corner, embraces Christmas in a way unlike any other. Here, the southern hemisphere's summer transforms the traditional wintery Christmas themes into a brilliantly unique, sunlit version. This distinct approach weaves together an intricate tapestry of cultural adaptability, local ingenuity, and international influences, making it a yuletide destination worth exploring.

In Sydney, the festive season starts with a palpable excitement in the air as the city gears up for its iconic events. The festivities often kick off with the annual lighting of the Martin Place Christmas Tree. Adorning this central business district location, the tree becomes a beacon of celebration, meticulously decorated with thousands of lights and ornaments that capture the city's festive spirit. Crowds gather, their faces illuminated by the dazzling display, as choirs fill the air with classic carols, kickstarting the season of joy and goodwill. It's a communal event where the magic of Christmas encourages strangers to share smiles and stories under the twinkling Australian sky.

One of the most talked-about features of Sydney's Christmas is the juxtaposition of traditional yuletide symbols with an undeniable local twist. Imagine Santa trading his sleigh for a surfboard, riding the waves at Bondi Beach—a scene that embodies Sydney's laid-back and adventurous approach to life. This annual surf event attracts visitors and locals alike, eager to watch the jolly old man tackle Australia's legendary surf alongside a group of similarly clad Santas, all in the name of charity and festive cheer.

Sydney's festive offerings also extend to an array of outdoor markets that spring up around the city, each with its own charm and specialty. These markets provide a platform for local artisans and producers to showcase their wares in an environment that's as lively as it is festive. The atmosphere at the Rocks Christmas Markets, for instance, is particularly enchanting. Nestled in one of the oldest neighborhoods, shrouded in history and cobblestone streets, this market offers unique gifts, handmade crafts, and gourmet food that reflect both Sydney's cultural diversity and its culinary innovation. Visitors can find everything from Indigenous artwork to modern

Australian cuisine, making it an ideal spot to pick up a meaningful gift or enjoy a delightful meal.

Feeling peckish? Sydney's cuisine during the holidays is also a delightful exploration of taste, where traditional Christmas dishes are reimagined to suit the summer season. Picture a lavish feast set against a backdrop of blue skies and ocean breezes—seafood plays a starring role, with fresh prawns, oysters, and fish often gracing the table, replacing the heavier winter roasts and stews. Outdoor barbecues become a popular festive gathering, where families and friends come together to celebrate under the open skies, with the sizzle of seafood and laughter mingling in the warm, summer air.

Sydney doesn't forget its younger attendees during this festive time. The city boasts a range of family-friendly activities designed to engage and entertain the little ones. Christmas Wonderland in Darling Harbour is a must-visit, with its enchanting array of lights, amusement rides, and interactive exhibits. It's a place where children can let their imaginations run wild, moving between the play areas, holiday workshops, and mesmerizing light displays that narrate the Christmas story in a way that's uniquely Australian.

From the Botanical Gardens to the shores of the Harbour, another remarkable feature of Sydney's Christmas celebrations is the harmonious integration of cultural festivities. As a multicultural city, Sydney embraces the richness of its diverse communities, inviting everyone to share their unique holiday traditions. Cultural festivals and performances occur throughout the month, blending music, dance, and storytelling from around the world. It's not uncommon to find festive food stalls offering everything from Italian panettone to Filipino bibingka, serving as a delicious reminder of Sydney's rich tapestry of cultures.

Then there's the quintessential experience of a Christmas cruise in Sydney Harbour. Families, travelers, and locals alike are drawn to the water to take in the iconic views—the Sydney Opera House, Harbour Bridge, and vibrant skyline—as they shimmer with festive lights. These cruises offer a tranquil escape from the hustle, where passengers can soak in the holiday ambiance with a chilled drink in hand, and perhaps spot New Year's fireworks rehearsal light up the night sky. It's a unique way to engage with the city's landscape, mixing leisurely sightseeing with the jovial spirit of the season.

Throughout the month of December, Sydney's various neighborhoods become alive with local festivities, fostering a strong community spirit. It is in these moments, where residents decorate their streets and homes or host local parades featuring community groups and schools, that Sydney's heart truly shines. Notable are Grants in the Grounds at Centennial Park, where a family-friendly festival celebrates local talents and crafts, reinforcing the sentiments of togetherness and community support.

Ultimately, Sydney's Christmas celebrations are a testament to the city's vibrant, ever-evolving identity. Here, the harmony between sunlit beaches, bustling markets, and culturally diverse communities creates a festive season enriched by tradition, yet refreshingly contemporary. It's a destination where one can experience the heartwarming familiarity of Christmas, wrapped in the invigorating zest of a summer celebration—an invitation to experience the warmth and wonder of Christmas in a way that only Sydney can offer. Whether you're a traveler drawn by curiosity or a holiday lover at heart, Sydney's unique celebrations promise memories that will linger long after the final Christmas light is dimmed.

Melbourne's Festive Traditions

While much of the world is blanketed in snow during the festive season, Melbourne offers a unique twist with its sun-kissed streets and vibrant holiday ambiance. The city's approach to celebrating

Christmas blends traditional Yuletide elements with its own distinctive charm, making it a must-visit destination for holiday enthusiasts. Imagine strolling through markets bursting with local produce, artisanal crafts, and cultural performances—all under the dazzling Australian sun.

Melbourne's festive traditions are a fusion of old and new, with a lively and colorful backdrop. Each year, the city transforms its metropolitan landscape into a festive wonderland. Central to this transformation is the much-celebrated Christmas Festival, where the city comes alive with events, parades, and light installations. One can wander through the festive arches of the Christmas Square at Federation Square, which hosts a magnificent display of lights and decorations. This central hub of festive activity brims with Christmas cheer as friends and families gather to enjoy live music, food stalls, and interactive installations.

The city's Christmas markets are a sensory delight, offering everything from handcrafted ornaments to gourmet food. A stroll through these markets may present opportunities to sample delicious mince pies, taste the rich flavors of a pavlova—a cherished Australian dessert—or sip on a glass of chilled sparkling wine. For those with a penchant for discovering unique gifts, the markets teem with local artisans showcasing their creativity through a variety of handcrafted goods.

Queen Victoria Market, an iconic Melbourne landmark, transforms into a bustling festive market during the holiday season. Known for its eclectic assortment of vendors, it becomes even more magical with twinkling fairy lights and special holiday stalls. It's a place where visitors can meander through aisles brimming with local produce, artisanal crafts, and festive treats. An evening visit to this market promises not just shopping, but a lively cultural experience with musical performances and children's activities.

Beyond the markets, Melbourne's festive traditions include several large-scale public events that capture the city's celebratory spirit. **Carols by Candlelight** is one such beloved tradition, bringing together thousands at the Sidney Myer Music Bowl. This iconic event has been running for decades, weaving beautiful melodies and the warmth of community spirit into an unforgettable night under the stars. Singers, musicians, and performers join hands with attendees, lighting up the evening with renditions of cherished Christmas classics.

Moreover, the city's streets come alive with dynamic events like the annual **Myer Christmas Parade**. Floats adorned with glittering decorations, performances inspired by beloved Christmas tales, and lively bands give life to the city center. This parade is not merely an event but a cherished tradition that draws crowds from all over the region, eager to partake in the joyful spectacle.

In Melbourne, Christmas isn't just about the events and festivities, it's also about the spirit of giving and community bonding. Many neighborhoods host events that showcase this ethos, such as festive charity walks and community fairs. These events serve as platforms for residents and visitors alike to contribute to causes aimed at supporting those in need, reinforcing the message of goodwill central to the season.

Another tradition that reflects Melbourne's unique approach to Christmas is the city's love for outdoor festivities. Given the warm weather, alfresco dining becomes a popular choice during the holiday season. Restaurants and cafes extend their dining spaces to the streets and laneways, offering festive menus that highlight both Australian and international flavors. It's common to find special holiday brunches or dinners featuring fresh seafood, barbecued meats, and a wide array of indulgent desserts.

For those drawn to artistic expressions of the festive season, Melbourne doesn't disappoint. The National Gallery of Victoria frequently hosts exhibitions that capture the spirit of Christmas, allowing visitors to explore varied interpretations of the holiday through art. Simultaneously, smaller galleries and art spaces throughout the city present an array of seasonal displays, providing an enriching cultural counterpoint to the more traditional events.

The approach of New Year's extends the festive atmosphere in Melbourne well beyond Christmas Day. The city's vibrant scene ensures there's something for everyone—from family-friendly events to lively parties that extend into the early hours. Fireworks over the Yarra River create a mesmerizing backdrop, marking the culmination of Melbourne's festive celebrations.

Ultimately, Melbourne's festive traditions represent more than just a season; they're a celebration of community, culture, and the joy of togetherness. The city's unique blend of traditional and contemporary festivities ensures a vibrant holiday experience that's cherished by locals and visitors alike. Whether you're joining the crowd at a bustling market, relaxing at a beachside Christmas picnic, or enjoying the spectacle of a parade, Melbourne invites you to partake in its sunny version of Yuletide magic.

Chapter 22:
New Zealand's Seasonal Blend

Amidst the Southern Hemisphere's midsummer embrace, New Zealand transforms its festive spirit into a rich tapestry of traditions, celebrating Christmas in its own unique style. In Auckland, the cityscape is alive with vibrant colors and Antipodean cheer. The markets bustle with a blend of familiar and novel aromas—gingerbread mingles with the scent of fresh ocean breezes, while local artisans display handmade crafts that tell stories of both Maori heritage and contemporary life. Moving down to Wellington, the windswept capital, the festivities take on a distinctive character. Here, the rhythm of the city is punctuated by merry gatherings where locals and visitors alike dive into culinary delights, from barbecue feasts to traditional mince pies with a Kiwi twist. It's a holiday experience where the joy of connection and the beauty of the land come together, offering travelers a refreshing departure from the typical winter wonderland, yet still capturing the heartwarming essence of the season.

Auckland's Antipodean Celebrations

As the sun ushers in warmth and vibrancy down under, Auckland embraces a unique festive spirit that's quite unlike the snowy festivities in the Northern Hemisphere. Christmas in New Zealand coincides with summer, flipping traditional holiday imagery upside down and offering travelers a Christmas experience that's undeniably distinctive. Picture this: instead of snowfall, Auckland's skies promise long sunny days, where light bounces off glistening beaches. The sprawling city becomes a hub of excitement and diverse holiday celebrations—across its coastal shores, bustling markets, and verdant parks.

In Auckland, the essence of Christmas is both familiar and refreshingly different. Here, the season is embodied by the blooming pohutukawa trees—a Kiwi Christmas staple. Known as New Zealand's Christmas tree, these stunning flora explode into vibrant reds, matching the holiday hues seen worldwide. Stroll along the Auckland waterfront, and you're likely to see these striking trees decorating the cityscape, a natural spectacle that's cherished by locals and intriguing to visitors.

When it comes to festive markets, Auckland certainly doesn't disappoint. The city hosts a variety of Christmas markets that showcase local artisans, culinary wonders, and Kiwi hospitality. Set against the backdrop of Auckland's iconic Sky Tower, the markets buzz with energy, offering everything from handcrafted gifts to gourmet food trucks serving up delightful local fare. Here, you can taste the true flavors of New Zealand. Don't be surprised to find stalls selling pavlova, a beloved meringue dessert topped with fresh fruits, often served as the centerpiece of a New Zealand Christmas feast.

Auckland's markets are a sensory delight, enriched by the sounds of carolers, which blend harmoniously with the soft strums of guitars—a nod to New Zealand's rich musical heritage. Here, visitors experience a tapestry of cultural performances, where traditional Maori haka dances might share the stage with contemporary Kiwi bands. This blend of the old and new, the traditional and modern, creates a dynamic cultural experience.

Wandering these vibrant markets, you'll inevitably be drawn to the local arts and crafts stalls. Artisan craftspeople proudly display their wares, each product a testament to skill and creativity. From intricately carved wooden items to beautiful woven baskets and jewelry, these markets are a fantastic place to find unique gifts with a personal touch. Many of these artisans draw inspiration from the natural beauty surrounding them, offering goods that tell the story of New Zealand's land and its people.

Beyond the markets, Auckland comes alive with community events and festivities. Parades are a big part of the scene, where floats bedecked with twinkling lights travel through the city's streets, children squealing with delight at the sight of Santa in his summer attire. These events are not just about spectacle; they are about bringing people together, celebrating in the true spirit of Christmas with warmth and camaraderie—even if that warmth is mostly from the sun.

For travelers seeking a quieter holiday experience, Auckland's surrounding nature reserves and beaches offer a more tranquil retreat. Here, one can witness the Christmas spirit conveyed through leisurely picnics on sandy shores, family barbecues sizzling under the sun, and serene boat rides on the Hauraki Gulf. Aucklanders trade in the traditional Christmas turkey for fresh seafood cooked on the grill, echoing the laid-back Kiwi lifestyle.

In Kakamatua Inlet, 40 minutes from the city center, families often gather with their dogs for some beach fun, making the most out of the warm weather while still cherishing time together. This blending of festivities with the outdoors echoes the core values of New Zealand's Christmas—a time of community, family, and gratitude for the stunning environment they inhabit.

Auckland also boasts a multicultural population, and this diversity shines through in its festive celebrations. Each community brings its flavors, traditions, and customs, adding a rich array of events throughout the season. From Diwali-inspired light displays to Chinese New Year performances later in the season, Auckland celebrates inclusivity, making anyone and everyone feel at home during the holidays.

The city's culinary scene further illustrates these diverse influences. Restaurants and pop-up eateries experiment with traditional holiday menus, incorporating local ingredients and flavors. Dishes combine Maori and Pacific Islander staples with European classics, offering a Christmas dinner that is as varied as it is delicious. Menus may feature anything from roast lamb to seafood feasts, all accompanied by New Zealand's renowned wines and craft beers.

As night falls, Auckland's festive lights take center stage, transforming the city into a sparkling wonderland. Locals and tourists alike flock to Franklin Road, famous for its impressive holiday light displays. Residents open their doors to share the festive cheer, where the streets are awash with color and creativity, each home a beacon of holiday spirit.

Auckland's Antipodean Christmas provides an experience that's truly unique—a place where sunshine meets holiday magic, and traditional festivities dance in harmony with the city's vibrant, multicultural identity. For those seeking to experience Christmas from a different perspective, Auckland offers sun-drenched memories and heartwarming community connections, redefining what the holiday season can mean.

Wellington's Windy Festivities

In New Zealand, where December is synonymous with summer, Wellington's Christmas market experiences bring a refreshing twist to traditional festivities. Known for its windy weather, Wellington seamlessly merges its natural elements with the festive spirit. The initially surprising mix of the city's blustery breezes and the warmth of Yuletide traditions creates a unique celebration that embraces the city's charm. Strolling through Wellington's bustling streets, visitors are greeted with vibrant decorations, the joyous sounds of holiday music, and the enticing smell of sizzling delicacies from market stalls.

Wellington's Christmas festivities unfold across different neighborhoods, each offering its distinct vibe. On one corner, you'll find the iconic Cuba Street, transformed into a lively theater of holiday cheer with its bohemian flair. Here, the market stalls glimmer under strings of lights, introducing shoppers to an array of handcrafted goods and artisanal products. There's an abundance of local crafts, from intricate jewelry to beautifully designed fabrics, reflecting the craftsmanship and creativity of New Zealand's artisans.

As you wander through the stalls, the aroma of mulled wine, albeit a chilled version perfect for the Southern Hemisphere's summer, blend with the enticing scents of local treats. The culinary offerings at Wellington's markets are a joyous exploration of flavors. You'll find traditional dishes with a Kiwi twist, including savory pies and barbecued meats, as well as pavlova adorned with fresh fruits—a nod to seasonal favorites.

The waterfront area, with its stunning views of Wellington Harbor, also hosts festivities that are both vibrant and serene. Here, the festivities are enhanced by the natural beauty surrounding them, offering a picturesque backdrop that inspires awe. It's not uncommon to find live music performances enhancing the lively atmosphere. Local bands and choirs fill the air with festive tunes, inviting passersby to pause and soak in the holiday spirit.

Wellington's whimsical weather is part of the city's charm, and locals embrace it with warmth and humor. On particularly windy days, the air is filled with laughter as hats are playfully snatched away by gusting winds, and market stalls flutter with festive decorations. It's all part of the experience—one that worldwide visitors come to cherish.

For those seeking a deeper cultural immersion, the city offers events showcasing Maori traditions and performances. These include haka displays and traditional carving demonstrations, presenting an authentic narrative of the region's cultural heritage. The integration of indigenous culture into the Christmas celebrations enriches the experience, adding layers of history and storytelling to the cheerful ambiance.

Wellington's communities also come together for festive events that enhance the inclusive spirit of the season. The Santa Parade, a beloved annual event, brings joyful anticipation as floats and performers traverse the streets, accompanied by the jolly man himself. Families gather to watch the spectacle unfold, their excitement mirrored in the twinkling fairy lights that line the avenues.

Another highlight is the iconic Christmas market in the Botanic Garden, where nature plays a key role in the festivities. Here, the market evolves into a magical evening event as night falls, and the garden's paths are illuminated with enchanting light displays. This interplay between nature and light creates a serene yet festive environment, inviting couples and families alike to wander through the illuminated tentacles of decorated trees.

The spirit of giving is also woven through Wellington's Christmas activities. There are numerous opportunities for visitors to participate in community initiatives, whether it is by attending charity events or contributing to local food drives. This collective generosity adds a meaningful dimension to the holiday cheer, reminding everyone of the shared joy in giving and receiving.

Nature lovers can take advantage of the city's stunning surroundings by embarking on festive-themed excursions. Trails and walkways offer scenic avenues for exploration, with many paths leading to vantage points that afford breathtaking views of the city, dressed in its holiday best. For those seeking a combination of adventure and festivity, there are guided tours that mix outdoor activities with holiday narratives, making for memorable experiences under the bright summer sun.

Wellington's windy festivities encapsulate the city's vibrant spirit and unique blend of cultures. The mingling of traditional Christmas elements with the country's own distinctive style results in an unforgettable celebration. Visitors leave with not only a treasure trove of experiences but also a sense of inspiration from the Kiwi way of commemorating the holidays—authentic, spirited, and entwined with nature.

With each market, parade, and cultural offering, Wellington proves that even in the warmth and wind of a Southern Hemisphere summer, the festive spirit of Christmas is as alive as ever. It's an experience that invites travelers to savor the moment and appreciate the diverse traditions that enrich their journey through New Zealand's capital.

Chapter 23:
Christmas Markets of the Middle East

In the heart of a region renowned for its rich history and vibrant cultures, the Christmas markets of the Middle East offer an unexpected yet enchanting twist on holiday traditions. Imagine strolling through Beirut, where the aroma of spiced coffee mingles with the scent of freshly baked baklava, creating an exotic festive atmosphere that delights the senses. Amman transforms into a kaleidoscope of lights, with local artisans showcasing their crafts, offering everything from intricate textiles to unique pottery. Here, east meets west in a delightful fusion that celebrates inclusivity and community spirit. The markets are not only a feast for the eyes but a tribute to shared celebrations where visitors are welcomed with open arms, giving travelers a sense of belonging amidst the festive buzz. This unique holiday experience invites you to immerse yourself in a blend of modern and traditional, where holiday cheer transcends borders and brings people together in joyous harmony. Discover a different side of the holiday season as you explore the creativity, warmth, and resilience of the Middle Eastern festive spirit.

Lebanon's Cultural Celebrations

Lebanon, with its rich tapestry of cultural and religious influences, offers a unique canvas on which its Christmas celebrations are painted. While Christmas markets are not traditionally Lebanese, the festive spirit that envelops this Mediterranean country is palpable during the holiday season. Lebanon's Christmas celebrations are not bound by extensive marketplaces like those in Europe; instead, they weave a story of community, tradition, and a vibrant mix of old and new.

In the heart of Beirut, the capital city of Lebanon, the holiday season is marked by a sparkling transformation. Streets are adorned with twinkling lights, echoing a contemporary urban sophistication mixed with heartfelt traditional practices. Beirut's Christmas decorations play a crucial role in setting the festive mood, inviting locals and tourists alike to revel in the city's dazzling display, especially around prominent areas like the Downtown district, which becomes a hub of holiday festivities.

Lebanon's distinct cultural celebrations during Christmas are deeply interwoven with its rich religious tapestry. With a significant Christian population, Lebanon sees jubilant church services and nativity plays that mark the holiday's spirituality, a core element of its festive season. The churches, many of which are historical landmarks in their own right, become the epicenter of solemn yet joyous gatherings. Each event at the church is not merely a religious obligation but a communal activity, bringing together people amidst the chants of hymns that tell stories as old as time.

However, Lebanese Christmas is not just about traditional church rituals. It is a vibrant mosaic where the traditional and the modern blend seamlessly. This is beautifully exemplified in the Lebanese culinary scene during Christmas. Households are bustling with preparations of festive meals, which form the backbone of celebrations. Visitors can indulge in tantalizing Lebanese dishes like stuffed grape leaves, kibbeh, and tabbouleh, culminating with desserts such as maamoul—sweet pastries filled with dates, nuts, or pistachios.

As the aroma of Lebanese Christmas delicacies wafts through homes and restaurants, marketplaces in cities like Byblos add another layer to the celebrations. Byblos, one of the world's oldest cities, hosts an enchanting blend of traditional markets and holiday-themed events. The city's ancient cobblestones lead you through a journey where history and festivity walk hand in hand, offering a visual feast—think vibrant stalls that showcase exquisite local crafts, aromatic spices, and traditional Lebanese delights.

The spirit of giving is a fundamental aspect of Christmas in Lebanon. Gift-giving, while not commercialized to the extent seen in Western counterparts, is cherished and personalized. Lebanese markets during this season offer unique handcrafted gifts that resonate with personal and cultural significance, reflecting the warmth with which gifts are exchanged among family and friends.

Moreover, the spirit of togetherness during the holidays shines bright across Lebanon. Communities come together, transcending religious differences, in a shared celebration of life, love, and hope. Various towns and villages organize holiday festivities like concerts and nativity exhibitions, further unifying people through shared experiences and fostering a deep sense of belonging.

Another highlight of Lebanese Christmas is the hospitality shown by its people. Whether in urban centers or rural settings, the hospitality extended by Lebanese families is legendary. You are likely to find yourself invited to a family gathering, where the conversation flows as freely as the local Araq, a traditional anise-flavored spirit. The sense of community and the warmth of Lebanese hospitality leave a lasting impression, providing travelers with memories they cherish long after they've left.

Finally, the natural beauty of Lebanon adds an extra dimension to Christmas celebrations. The country's diverse landscape, from the snow-capped mountains to the azure Mediterranean Sea, offers a picturesque backdrop that complements the festive spirit. This harmonious blend of nature and celebration creates an enchanting atmosphere where one can escape the hustle of city life and indulge in peaceful reflection or thrilling adventures.

Lebanon's Christmas celebrations uniquely embody joy, inclusivity, and reverence for tradition, offering a vivid cultural experience that enchants and inspires. Enjoying the Christmas season in Lebanon means immersing yourself in a destination where every corner is rich in history, generosity, and vibrant festivity.

Jordan's Festive Discoveries

Beyond its iconic deserts and ancient ruins, Jordan is redefining the holiday landscape with its own brand of Christmas market magic. While the Middle East may not be the first place that comes to mind when you think of winter wonderlands, Jordan's festive scene offers a captivating blend of Western traditions and local culture. Whether you're wandering through bustling streets adorned with twinkling lights or sampling holiday treats with a Middle Eastern twist, the experience is as unique as it is enchanting.

Amman, Jordan's vibrant capital, is the epicenter of these celebrations. As December unfolds, the city's neighborhoods transform into pockets of holiday cheer, each uniquely contributing to the city's festive mosaic. The markets are a sensory feast, where the spicy aroma of freshly brewed cardamom coffee mingles with the sweetness of traditional pastries like baklava, adding depth to the yuletide atmosphere.

The *Souk Jara*, a popular local market during the warmer months, turns itself into a wintery wonder as Christmas approaches. Known for its artisanal crafts and homegrown goods, it seamlessly takes on a new life as a Christmas market. This transformation brings with it decorations that integrate both local characteristics and international Christmas symbols, showcasing Jordan's ability to blend together various cultures while maintaining a distinct identity. Handmade ornaments, jewelry, and intricate textiles reflect the skills and stories of local artisans, each stall telling a different tale of heritage and craftsmanship.

What makes Jordan's festive offerings stand out are the interactive experiences. Among the most beloved is the live nativity scene, which features performances that recount the Christmas story in a style deeply rooted in the Middle Eastern narrative tradition. It's not uncommon to see locals and tourists alike participating in these reenactments, creating a shared cultural moment that resonates with visitors from all over the world.

Evenings in Amman become particularly magical when the city hosts its annual Christmas carol concerts. These events have grown in popularity and feature a mix of traditional carols and contemporary Middle Eastern interpretations. Churches and community centers open their doors, fostering a spirit of inclusiveness, where all are welcome to join in the celebration. This melding of musical styles highlights Jordan's diverse cultural landscape, appealing to both the young and the old, transcending language and religious differences.

Food, of course, plays a central role. Stalls at the markets offer a delightful array of festive fare, from traditional Christmas cookies to dishes with a distinct local flair. Imagine indulging in *mansaf*, Jordan's national dish of lamb and rice, seasoned with holiday spices. Or savoring warm dates stuffed with rich nuts, their sweetness providing comfort on the cooler winter nights. Each bite is a reminder of the region's abundant hospitality and flavor.

In addition to the capital, other cities in Jordan, like Irbid and Madaba, also partake in the holiday spirit, although on a smaller scale. These markets tend to be more intimate, attracting local families and curious travelers. Within these communities, you find a genuine exchange of holiday traditions, where neighbors share recipes, stories, and the warmth of the season, embodying the true spirit of Christmas.

Winter Wonderlands

Public squares and parks often host open-air movies that showcase holiday classics, providing an opportunity for families to gather under the stars with steaming mugs of cinnamon-infused tea. Meanwhile, children giggle and run around in designated play areas, where they can meet Santa Claus, a beloved icon who crosses cultural boundaries. These gatherings are not only about shopping and entertainment; they foster community and create lasting memories for young ones living in a region not typically associated with snowy celebrations.

It's important to note that Christmas in Jordan is more than a spectacle; it's a reflection of the country's deep-rooted ethos of coexistence and respect for different faiths. The significance of the holiday is not lost amidst the festivities, as it aligns well with Jordan's tradition of hospitality and its role as a historical crossroads of different civilizations and beliefs.

Travelers who experience Jordan during the holiday season often leave with a newfound respect for how this region celebrates diversity in unity. Beyond the biblical sites awaiting pilgrims in Bethlehem just across the border, Jordan offers kindred experiences with its own flair. It's an opportunity to witness how universal celebrations are interpreted with remarkable creativity and a deep respect for traditions, both new and ancient.

As the night sky darkens, wandering through Jordan's Christmas markets feels like strolling through a tale of both discovery and nostalgia. You're not merely visiting a market; you're stepping into a narrative woven with cultural threads that are as diverse as the wares for sale. The festive markets of Jordan showcase the country's ability to surprise and enchant, providing a perfect blend of merriment and meaning. In every twinkling light and cheerful smile, you feel the warmth that Jordan offers, redefining the holiday spirit in this enchanting corner of the world.

Chapter 24:
Africa's Unique Festive Traditions

In Africa, the holiday season is a vibrant tapestry woven with diverse cultural threads, offering a festive experience unlike any other. From the sunlit streets of South Africa, where Christmas markets brim with local crafts and savory delights, to the bustling souks of Morocco adorned with an eclectic blend of festive decor, the continent embraces the holiday spirit with unique flair. Visitors can indulge their senses with the rhythmic beats of traditional music and the tantalizing aromas of regional cuisine, creating a symphony of celebration amid stunning landscapes. Whether exploring a beachside market or a historic town center, Africa's festive traditions invite travelers to experience the warmth of a community that celebrates unity, heritage, and joyous gatherings under a shared sky. The continent's diverse festivities are a reminder of the universal joy that the holiday season brings, embodying a spirit of togetherness that transcends borders and cultures.

South Africa's Sunlit Markets

The idea of a Christmas market in the blazing summer sun of South Africa might sound paradoxical to those who equate the festive season with snowflakes and hot cocoa by the fireplace. Yet, South Africa offers a truly unique and vibrant twist on the traditional holiday market, embracing the warmth and sunshine that define a southern hemisphere Christmas.

Winter Wonderlands

Nestled in the heart of the country, Johannesburg plays host to some of South Africa's most lively Christmas markets. Imagine strolling through a bustling market where the scent of Braai, a traditional barbeque, mingles with fresh summer blooms as opposed to the rich spices of mulled wine. These markets are outdoor celebrations that emphasize local crafts, foods, and the ever-present spirit of welcoming warmth. Each stall tells a story, from handmade Zulu beadwork to colorful Ndebele blankets, offering visitors not just items, but pieces of the country's rich cultural tapestry.

Standing at the crossroads between traditional African culture and modern influences, the markets are a feast for the senses. As you walk through, you might hear the rhythmic beats of a gumboot dance, the traditional sounds reverberating through the summer air, inviting everyone to join in the celebration. Sellers passionately explain the stories behind their crafts, eager to share both culture and heritage with travelers seeking a deeper connection to the places they visit.

One cannot visit a South African Christmas market without indulging in its gastronomic delights. The markets explode with flavors that reflect both the diversity and creativity of South African cuisine—think bobotie and bunny chow rather than gingerbread and fruitcake. The fiery Durban curries available from a vendor-born and bred in KwaZulu-Natal are a highlight, as are the Cape Malay koeksisters with their sweet, syrup-soaked dough. Food in these markets is not just sustenance but a cultural exchange, with each bite offering insight into South Africa's melting pot of traditions.

Over in Cape Town, the Christmas markets present a slightly different flavor. Here, the backdrop of Table Mountain adds a dramatic touch to the sunlit stalls and merry gatherings. The air is filled with the smell of the ocean, mingling with the fragrance of local fynbos flowers sold at beautifully decorated stalls. The Cape Town markets, including the popular Kirstenbosch Craft and Food Market, emphasize sustainability and eco-friendly practices, aligning with the city's progressive ethos. Artisans focus on using locally-sourced materials, producing everything from clothing to toys, and even gourmet goods.

While Europeans might reach for a hot cup of cocoa, South Africans sip refreshing iced rooibos or delight in a craft beer from a local brewery as they explore these markets. The relaxed atmosphere invites lengthy conversations under blue skies, perhaps over a call into a heated game of African checkers or a curious chat surrounding the intricate details of a crafted ostrich egg.

Children experience the true magic of these markets through interactive storytelling and puppet shows, often featuring themes of African folklore. It's not uncommon for a market visit to culminate in a spontaneous sing-along. The children's eyes light up with the tales of Anansi the Spider or the adventures of other beloved folk heroes, sparking imaginations under summer skies rather than the glow of Christmas lights.

Unique to South Africa, the markets also host numerous community-focused causes. Many vendors are involved in social enterprises, and purchases often directly support local schools or healthcare initiatives. For visitors, this adds an extra layer of heart to the already warm atmosphere, turning shopping into a shared act of goodwill that resonates with the festive season's spirit of giving.

Though it's half a world away from the European holiday scenes, South Africa's sunlit markets embrace universal festive traditions: a community coming together, shared joy and laughter, and the giving and receiving of small treasures. All of these are fused with local customs, making for an experience that's both familiar and refreshingly different.

As twilight begins to fall, the stalls take on a golden hue, and the heat of the day settles into balmy evening warmth. This is when the markets become truly magical. Strings of fairy lights twinkle from stand to stand, and the gentle hum of conversation fills the air, suggesting that while snow might be absent, the spirit of Christmas is very much alive.

The experience at South Africa's markets leaves a lasting impression on visitors. It is a reminder that festive joy transcends temperature and climate, living instead in the shared smiles, laughter, and traditions that make this season special, no matter where you are in the world. By embracing the strengths of both their cultural identity and their sunny climate, the South African markets offer a festive flair entirely their own, promising memories as warm and unique as the African sun itself.

Morocco's Cultural Blend

In the heart of North Africa, Morocco stands as a mesmerizing tapestry of cultural diversity, where traditional Berber, Arab, and French influences blend seamlessly into a vibrant and colorful festive experience. Despite being a predominantly Muslim country, Morocco embraces the spirit of togetherness and celebration that characterizes the Christmas season, offering unique opportunities for travelers to experience an alternative kind of holiday festivity. Wandering through the bustling markets and aromatic souks, visitors can feel an undeniable festive energy, one enriched by centuries of cultural exchange.

Intriguingly diverse, Morocco's festive season isn't confined to traditional Christmas markets, but rather unfolds across the souks and city squares in ways that spotlight its rich heritage. Cities like Marrakech, Fes, and Casablanca come alive with bustling activity as artisans and craftsmen prepare to showcase their handmade goods. The vibrant hustle and bustle of the markets transform into living theatres of cultural expression. Here, travelers can encounter an eclectic mix of goods, from intricately woven rugs to beautifully crafted pottery, providing an insight into the mastery behind Moroccan craftsmanship.

The holiday season in Morocco is punctuated by the profusion of culinary delights that bridge the gap between tradition and festivity. Moroccan cuisine, famous worldwide for its bold flavors and rich textures, takes on special significance during this time. Stalls and street vendors offer a sampling of seasonal treats; imagine the warm sweetness of honey-drenched sweets that melt in your mouth or the tantalizing aroma of cumin-spiced harira soup simmering gently in the cool evening air. The culinary journey is as much about taste as it is about tradition, often bringing families together to share meals that have been passed down through generations.

Throughout December, the urban landscapes of Morocco exhibit a striking transformation. Lantern-lit streets and palm-lined boulevards take on a warm, welcoming glow, as Moroccan lamps cast intricate shadows that dance in the night. These enchanting visuals are accompanied by the sounds of local musicians, whose haunting melodies echo through the narrow alleys, lending a magical quality to the scenic nighttime ambiance. It's not uncommon to encounter traditional Moroccan music infused with Western carols, a testament to the open-minded embrace of various cultural elements.

While Morocco may not have traditional Christmas trees, the country boasts a natural beauty that rivals any festive decorations. The snow-capped Atlas Mountains offer a glorious backdrop, framing the celebrations with natural elegance. Many visitors take the opportunity to venture into the mountains for a different kind of white Christmas. Skiing and trekking adventures provide a thrilling contrast to the urban festive activities, inviting travelers to explore Morocco's diverse landscapes that range from rugged peaks to vast desert expanses.

Local traditions are ever-present in the form of dance and folklore performances, where the tales of Morocco's storied past are brought to life. Traditional Berber music and dance, in particular, play an integral part in the cultural festivities, drawing visitors into a sophisticated tapestry of rhythm and movement. These performances not only celebrate the season but also highlight Morocco's commitment to preserving its rich heritage while embracing modern influences. It's a delicate balance that resonates through the years, captivating travelers and locals alike.

Gift-giving, although not traditionally Moroccan, finds its place in the festivities, offering travelers a chance to engage in the exchange of hand-made gifts. It's the perfect opportunity to share pieces of Moroccan artistry with loved ones, further intertwining personal experiences with cultural richness. The purchase of these artisanal items helps support local communities and ensure that craftsman skills are passed on to future generations, maintaining this unique cultural heritage.

For those looking to deepen their cultural understanding, exploring historic sites during the holiday season is equally rewarding. Morocco's architectural gems, such as the grand mosques and ancient kasbahs, are steeped in history and offer a contemplative retreat from the crowded markets. These sites provide a backdrop to the season's merriment while inviting visitors to reflect on the broader narratives of Morocco's cultural evolution. Walking through these timeworn corridors, one can appreciate the artistry and devotion that has shaped the country's identity over the centuries.

As night falls, the scent of aromatic spices and the sounds of distant celebrations create a sensory experience that is uniquely Moroccan. In towns and cities, the clamor of the day subsides into a gentle hum, and the crisp desert air is filled with starry possibilities. Here, tradition and modernity intertwine seamlessly, forming a narrative that speaks to Morocco's intrinsic ability to celebrate both its past and present. The experience is not just festive, but deeply immersive, leaving an indelible mark on those fortunate enough to witness it.

Perhaps what is most enchanting about Morocco's winter wonderland is the sense of personal discovery it affords. Each souk, each conversation, and each taste is a small thread in a larger, more intricate story—a story of a nation that celebrates its diversity and change without losing sight of its roots. As travelers wander through the labyrinthine streets, uncovering layers of history and identity, they find themselves not only exploring a country but connecting with a vibrant, living tradition.

In essence, Morocco's cultural blend offers a festive experience that is refreshingly distinct and intimately memorable. Here, the holiday season is less about the trappings of Christmas as we know it and more about the inviting warmth of Moroccan hospitality, the beauty of its traditions, and the spirit of shared celebration that transcends borders. For those seeking a festive adventure that challenges their expectations and broadens their horizons, Morocco stands ready to welcome them into its captivating blend of cultures and celebrations.

Chapter 25: Embracing Christmas Markets Around the Globe

From the enchanting glow of twinkling lights in Europe to the sunlit bazaars of Africa, Christmas markets offer a tantalizing array of global traditions infused with modern flair. As you wander from one bustling market to the next, you'll find yourself immersed in a tapestry of festive melodies, artisanal crafts, and culinary delights that span continents. Picture savoring roasted chestnuts in a centuries-old plaza in Prague, then marveling at inventive holiday displays in Tokyo's high-tech streets. In every market, there is a shared spirit of celebration that transcends borders, offering a glimpse into the cultures and customs that make each destination unique. The warmth of handcrafted gifts and the sweet aroma of spiced mulled wine invite travelers to embrace the season's magic, fostering connections with locals and other wanderers alike. Each experience becomes a chapter of its own, contributing to the larger story of how Christmas markets, with their rich histories and evolving traditions, unite us in a global celebration of joy.

Uniting Winter Festivals

The chill of winter has a way of bringing people together in ways that few other seasons can. Across the globe, as temperatures drop, spirits rise, and communities come alive with the joyous chaos of winter festivals. Though Christmas markets are the hallmark of these seasonal celebrations, many cultures incorporate unique elements that transcend geographic and cultural boundaries, creating a global canvas of unity through celebration.

One striking similarity among these festivals is their ability to transform ordinary urban spaces into wonderlands of festive cheer. Think about the twinkling lights of Strasbourg, the snow-laden squares of Moscow, or the sunny but equally dazzling decorations in Sydney. Each market, regardless of its location, shares a common goal: to enchant, to inspire, and most importantly, to unite individuals across all walks of life through shared experiences. It's a universal theme that echoes the spirit of community—a key element in every global winter festival.

In the heart of Europe, where these markets often find their most traditional forms, a multitude of nations serve as both a canvas and an artist in this seasonal masterpiece. Countries like Germany, Austria, and France showcase an array of wooden stalls filled with handcrafted toys, aromatic mulled wines, and comforting foods that are as endearing as they are diverse. Yet, as you traverse into the Nordic realms, you'll notice how they add their own cultural twists. Here, the markets vibrate with the resonance of local folklore and myth, making them an integral part of the region's yuletide magic.

Moving beyond Europe, North America's vibrant take on these markets provides a new layer of excitement and diversity. Whether it's the iconic Rockefeller Center market in New York or the multicultural atmosphere of Chicago's Christkindlmarket, there is a palpable energy that embraces both tradition and modernity. These markets have a way of blending various cultural elements, naturally reflecting the melting pot nature of these societies and celebrating the congregation of diverse backgrounds under the winter's embrace.

In Asia, winter festivals have a distinctive character, beautifully blending international influences with local traditions. Tokyo's

Winter Wonderlands

dazzling illuminations and Seoul's elaborate festive displays cast the cities in a magical light. These celebrations not only showcase the region's knack for adopting elements from different cultures but also underline their own unique festive interpretations, resulting in an enchanting mix of east meets west.

Meanwhile, in the southern hemisphere, cities like Melbourne and Auckland cleverly invert the traditional Christmas market by mixing it with summer festivities, showing that the spirit of togetherness transcends conventional expectations. New Zealand and Australia's markets, with their sunny yet cozy environments, maintain that festive spark by uniting communities in a celebration unique to their geographical identity.

Many of these winter festivals extend their reach beyond the commercial aspect, engaging in cultural exchanges, showcasing traditional performances, or even benevolent activities like charity events. For instance, markets in countries such as Poland and Czech Republic often host displays of nativity plays, and choirs sing age-old carols, further deepening the cultural resonance and shared joy among attendees.

Let's not overlook how these winter festivals adapt to meet the needs of an ever-evolving world. Sustainability plays an increasingly critical role, with many markets turning towards eco-friendly decorations and stalls serving locally-sourced products. It's not just a shift in operations; it's a conscious effort to form a deeper connection with the environment and ensure that future generations can also revel in this magical time of year.

Indeed, the simultaneous familiarity and novelty found in various winter festivals are what make them fascinating to both new and seasoned visitors. It's a dance between past and present, a fusion of timeless customs and contemporary innovations. Markets across the globe offer an opportunity to delve into an experience that is as culturally enriching as it is heartwarming, embodying a microcosm of our world's diversity in the spirit of the season.

At the heart of it all, winter festivals are a testament to the human spirit's capacity for warmth and unity amid the year's coldest months. They remind us of the joys of shared experiences and the importance of coming together to celebrate community, diversity, and tradition, no matter where in the world we find ourselves. It's these shared bonds that truly unite winter festivals, weaving a tapestry of global goodwill and festive cheer that transcends borders and brings us closer together in celebration of life itself.

Global Traditions and Modern Twists

Christmas markets worldwide have long been intertwined with age-old traditions, but they're not immune to the progression of time. Iconic seasonal practices are finding fresh forms in cultures spread across the globe, creating a beautiful tapestry of past and present. The magic of these markets isn't just about the nostalgia tied to them; it's how they embrace both old-world charm and innovative celebrations, inviting visitors to experience the blend in every corner of the world.

In many ways, the evolution of Christmas markets is less about replacing tradition and more about breathing new life into it. From handcrafted wooden toys to digital light shows, vendors and organizers are seamlessly integrating the conventional with the contemporary. In historic European capitals, for instance, century-old market squares host light displays projected onto ancient buildings, marrying heritage architecture with cutting-edge technology. It's a dance between conserving culture and embracing modern creativity, creating an atmosphere that captivates both the heart and the senses.

France offers a compelling example of this fusion. The snow-clad Alsatian town of Strasbourg, touted as the capital of Christmas, takes pride in its deep-rooted holiday customs. Yet, amid its charming wooden huts laden with roasted chestnuts and mulled wine, you might find pop-up experiences elevating the spirit. These temporary setups introduce interactive displays and culinary innovations, drawing visitors into an immersive festive world where past and present harmonize perfectly.

Meanwhile, across the Atlantic, North American markets have borrowed the essence of European traditions but added their creative interpretation. Take a stroll through New York City, and you might stumble upon a vendor offering hot apple cider next to a stall selling gingerbread with a twist — think infused with espresso or matcha. Not merely a transaction between buyer and seller, these interactions become cultural exchanges where every mug or ornament tells a story with a dash of modern flair.

In Amsterdam, the picturesque streets echo with laughter and music, as has been the way for decades. Yet, there's something new in the air — a contemporary jazz band playing alongside carol singers offers a fresh auditory experience. While the canal-side glühwein stands aren't going anywhere, the inclusion of such inventive elements shows a dynamic acceptance of change, ensuring these markets remain relevant to younger generations without alienating traditionalists.

Australia provides another fascinating juxtaposition. With its unique summer Christmas, the markets here have embraced the sunny climes while maintaining their yuletide spirit. Markets in Melbourne and Sydney combine local flavors like lamingtons and pavlova with classic Christmas puddings, presenting a delightful culinary blend. The introduction of immersive VR experiences, where visitors take a virtual sleigh ride through a snow-draped European town, is a testament to their innovative approach, making winter wonderlands accessible in the 80-degree heat.

Similarly, in Asia, the blend of local traditions with Christmas vibes offers a captivating market experience. In Japan, the renowned winter illuminations draw throngs of locals and tourists alike, combining the country's penchant for innovation with festive cheer. Although Christmas isn't a traditional holiday in Japan, the markets have carved a niche, focusing on light-hearted enjoyment and decorative elegance inspired by both Japanese and Western influences.

Heading to the Middle East, markets in cities like Beirut are showcasing a remarkable cultural intertwine. Christmas might not be predominantly observed in Lebanon, yet the markets buzz with cross-cultural enthusiasm. Traditional Middle Eastern crafts sit comfortably next to imported Christmas goods, giving a nod to both regionally crafted beauty and globally recognized festive trends. The addition of live storytelling and music from different ethnic backgrounds adds an enriching layer.

Modern twists aren't just for the urban marketplaces; some rural areas are bringing their A-game to this global celebration. In Poland, moving away from hubs like Krakow, smaller towns are organizing Christmas markets interwoven with digital storytelling. Projected onto rustic barns and farmhouses, these stories draw from folklore, infusing these lesser-known locales with an enchanting modern energy.

Even in South America, where Christmas falls during the height of summer, markets have embraced this seasonal anomaly, offering beachside festivities complete with local music and dance. Brazil has innovated its Christmas festivals by introducing dynamic cultural parades that weave through the market streets, merging religious traditions with vibrant samba rhythms, leaving a lasting impression on those fortunate enough to witness them.

The global landscape continues to offer fascinating new takes on how this beloved tradition is celebrated, providing travelers with endless opportunities for discovery. Whether wandering through the snowy streets of Eastern Europe or sipping mulled cider under Australia's blazing sun, Christmas markets today are about exploring the endless possibilities where history and innovation collide. These unique blends create an inviting spirit of unity — a perfect reflection of Christmas itself, which despite cultural boundaries, has evolved into a universal celebration.

Ultimately, the most significant charm of Christmas markets lies in their ability to weave global traditions with modern twists, transforming familiar spaces into unexpected delights. Wherever you find yourself, the spirit of these markets reaffirms one thing: that joy and goodwill are at the heart of this shared human experience, accessible in myriad ways across the globe.

Conclusion

The journey through the world's Christmas markets has been nothing short of enchanting. Each destination unfolded like a beautifully wrapped gift, offering its own distinct traditions and festive splendor. These markets are not just places to shop; they are vibrant celebrations of culture, history, and community. As we delve deeper into the interconnectedness of these festivities, it becomes clear that, despite geographical boundaries, the spirit of Christmas markets resonates universally.

The magic of European markets, from the warm glow of Germany's Nuremberg to the artisanal charm of Italy's Florence, sets the stage for an unforgettable winter wonderland. You could stroll through Austria's Vienna, where the air is filled with the scent of roasted chestnuts, or get lost in the captivating lights of France's Strasbourg. These places remind us of the deep-rooted traditions and the joy of shared experiences that define the European festive season.

Beyond Europe, the Christmas spirit travels beyond continents, embracing diverse cultures and climates. Picture the bustling energy of New York's iconic markets alongside Tokyo's illuminated celebrations — both brimming with their own cultural tapestries. It's a testament to how Christmas markets adapt and thrive, weaving a vibrant global tapestry without losing their essence.

In discovering each market, we've explored a world where past meets present and tradition meets innovation. From the Nordic countries where the dark winter months transform into snowy festivities, to the sunny celebrations of Australia's Sydney or South Africa, we see how each place brings its unique twist to a shared tradition. This diversity yet familiarity offers travelers not just a holiday destination but a heartfelt, global embrace.

For the travel enthusiast and holiday lover, these markets serve as a bridge — connecting cultures, forging friendships, and creating memories that last a lifetime. The festive stalls, cozy atmospheres, and laughter filling the air all evoke a sense of wonder and nostalgic yearning, encouraging us to return each year to the warmth they offer.

As the last chapter draws to a close, the allure of Christmas markets has shown not only how they captivate our senses but how they offer an opportunity to learn, to connect, and to celebrate the universal joy that the holiday season brings. They've become more than seasonal attractions; they are a testament to the world's wonderful diversity and shared love for celebration.

In essence, Christmas markets around the globe invite us to pause and appreciate the season's beauty, whether we're sipping mulled wine in Prague or enjoying a festive concert in Buenos Aires. They urge us to look beyond the tangible goods on display and instead cherish the intangible: the joy, the community, and the connections forming amidst twinkling lights and joyous melodies.

So, as you prepare to explore these markets, carry with you the understanding that each visit enhances a richer appreciation of our world's cultures and traditions. Let the warmth of these market cities into your heart, and may the memories you've gathered inspire your travels with a renewed sense of wonder and gratitude. Let each market gift you a story, a moment, a new tradition to cherish, and the understanding that Christmas, in all its forms and festivities, is a universal celebration of togetherness and joy.

Appendix A: Appendix

Diving into the world of Christmas markets isn't just about joyous strolls amidst glittering lights and festive stalls; it's a journey enriched by understanding and respect for local traditions. As you wander through these seasonal wonderlands, it becomes essential to embrace not only the aromatic mulled wines and artisanal crafts but also the subtle nuances of cultural etiquette. Engaging with vendors in their native tongue, if possible, and adhering to customary greetings and gestures can further elevate your experience and forge genuine connections with the locals. Additionally, knowing the best times to visit and the must-try specialties exclusive to each market can turn a casual visit into an unforgettable adventure. This appendix serves as your compact guide, offering essential tips and insights that will enhance your global Christmas market explorations, ensuring your journeys are as respectful as they are delightful.

Tips for Visiting Christmas Markets

Visiting a Christmas market is like stepping into a winter wonderland filled with twinkling lights, the aroma of spiced mulled wine, and the harmonies of seasonal carols. These enchanting markets, each with its unique flair, are scattered across the globe, providing a special blend of tradition and festivity. Whether you're a seasoned Christmas market explorer or a first-time visitor, there are a few tips that can enhance your experience and help you immerse yourself fully in the magical atmosphere.

Before you embark on your festive journey, consider timing your visit to avoid the heaviest crowds. Midweek visits and early afternoon strolls can often mean thinner crowds, allowing you to take in the ambiance without the shoulder-to-shoulder hustle and bustle. On the other hand, if you're drawn to the energy and vibe of a bustling market, an evening trip to enjoy the markets aglow in lights can be quite magical. Just keep in mind that weekends tend to be the busiest.

Dressing appropriately cannot be overstated. Remember, many Christmas markets are set against a backdrop of chilly weather, so layering is key. A warm coat, hat, gloves, and perhaps a thermos of hot cocoa are indispensable for those trading the indoors for the brisk, frosty air. Don't underestimate comfortable footwear, either, as you'll likely be logging quite a bit of mileage on cobblestone paths and around snow-dusted stalls.

Timing your visit to coincide with specific events or performances can also enrich your experience. Many markets host live music, traditional puppet shows, or even appearances by Santa Claus himself. Check local listings or market announcements to see if there's anything special happening during your visit. These moments add a layer of local flavor and tradition that truly brings the market to life.

Sampling local cuisines and holiday treats is a quintessential part of any Christmas market visit. From bratwurst and gingerbread in Germany to roasted chestnuts in France, the variety of food can offer a delicious peek into local holiday traditions. Make it a mission to try at least one item that's new or unique to the region you're visiting. Many markets sell special holiday beverages like Glühwein or hot cider; these warm concoctions are perfect for sipping as you browse through the stalls.

Don't forget to wander off the beaten path within the market. While the central stalls often showcase local crafts and gifts, vendors in quieter corners might have hidden gems. Engaging with artisans and stallkeepers can provide unique insights into the making of their products, also offering you the chance to absorb the local culture more deeply. Purchasing an item directly from the maker creates a meaningful connection with both the piece and your travel experience.

Being mindful of cultural nuances and etiquette is important when visiting Christmas markets, especially if you're exploring them internationally. Simple gestures, like greeting vendors with "Frohe Weihnachten" in Germany or "Joyeux Noël" in France, can go a long way in making your interactions warm and welcoming. Respect any local customs or traditions you might encounter; these markets are reflections of local culture and heritage.

Plan your logistics carefully, especially if you're visiting multiple markets in a city or across different countries. Public transport can be a convenient way to get around bustling holiday towns, and many cities offer special lines or additional services during the festive season. Research is key here; understanding opening times and transport schedules can help you maximize your time and avoid missing something special.

Bringing along a tote or small backpack can be incredibly useful. Besides carrying essentials like your camera and wallet, you'll appreciate having somewhere to stash those spontaneous purchases and impulse buys. Some markets also promote eco-friendly practices, so having your own reusable bag means you do your part in supporting sustainability.

If you're traveling to multiple markets, try to document your experiences. Whether it's jotting down notes about a particularly delicious treat, taking photos of intricate decorations, or collecting little keepsakes like ticket stubs, these small mementos help capture the essence of your travels. Upon returning home, these collections often become cherished memories that bring a smile whenever you revisit them.

The joy of visiting Christmas markets often lies in the unexpected, so leave room for spontaneity. Wander down alleyways brightly lit with festive decorations, get lost in the melody of a busker playing holiday tunes, or linger over that last cup of mulled wine. Embrace these moments without a rigid plan; they often lead to the most memorable experiences.

Finally, immerse yourself in the spirit of the holiday season. Let the glittering lights, the festive music, and the contagious joy wash over you. Take the opportunity to slow down, enjoy the pleasant moments, and share the experience with loved ones or new friends. Christmas markets hold a certain magic that resonates with the heart and fills it with warmth and wonder.

Wherever your journey takes you, may these tips help in making your holiday adventures through the world's Christmas markets unforgettable. From the snow-kissed stalls of Europe to the sunny celebrations of the Southern Hemisphere, the spirit of the season is alive and waiting for those who seek it out.

Cultural Etiquette and Insights

When exploring the world's diverse Christmas markets, understanding cultural nuances can elevate the experience from a simple visit to a profound journey of discovery. Embarking on this festive globe-trotting adventure requires a curiosity not just for the vibrant stalls and enticing flavors, but also for the rich tapestry of traditions and societal norms woven into each market.

At the heart of European Christmas markets, such as those found in Germany, lies a deep-seated respect for customs that date back centuries. The markets are bustling centers of activity where locals and visitors alike gather to share in the spirit of the season. One essential aspect to remember is the significance of personal space and politeness. Germans typically appreciate a degree of formality in social greetings; a simple "Guten tag" or a respectful nod goes a long way in making connections.

Moving to other parts of Europe, like France, savoring the scintillating lights of Strasbourg or basking in Paris's elegant holiday ambiance requires an appreciation for subtlety and style. The French value quality in all things, from fashion to food to conversation. Mastering a few phrases in French not only garners warm smiles but can lead to richer interactions. "Bonjour" and "Merci" are particularly appreciated. In markets where festive wine flows abundantly, it's customary to engage in quaint chit-chat over a glass of vin chaud, soaking in the jovial atmosphere.

The United Kingdom's festive landscapes, such as London's Winter Wonderland, envelop visitors in a whirlwind of frosty fun and historical homage. English markets are unique in their blend of tradition and modernity. Here, queuing is a cultural touchstone that underscores respect and order. Regardless of the chill in the air, patience is seen as a virtue, transforming any wait into an opportunity to exchange festive stories with fellow visitors.

Heading north, the Nordic countries present a Yuletide experience steeped in natural wonder and minimalist charm. Sweden and Finland offer markets where nature and festivity coexist in harmony. In these settings, sustainability is often at the forefront. Taking reusable bags not only respects local customs but also aligns with a broader eco-conscious ethos prevalent throughout Scandinavia. Here, markets are more than places to shop; they're opportunities to revel under the seasonal splendor, often with the backdrop of snow-topped landscapes.

Winter Wonderlands

In the Mediterranean, Christmas markets in countries such as Greece and Turkey present a fascinating cultural blend, where rich history and vibrant traditions collide. When navigating these markets, it's vital to acknowledge the deeply rooted hospitality that characterizes the region. Engaging with vendors and locals often opens doors to intimate cultural exchanges, a chance to learn about festive stories passed down through generations. Offering a courteous "Efharisto" or "Teşekkür ederim" signifies gratitude and respect.

Jumping across the Atlantic to the Americas, markets reveal an intriguing mix of indigenous influences and modern Christmas lore. In the United States, iconic spots like New York City showcase a melting pot of festivities, where the hustle is part of the charm, and expressing holiday cheer is welcomed with open arms. Meanwhile, Toronto's holiday lights shimmer alongside multicultural celebrations, emphasizing Canada's mosaic. Here, a spirit of inclusion is prevalent; acknowledging diverse traditions with an open heart enhances the holiday magic.

Visiting Christmas markets in Asia, especially in places like Japan and South Korea, introduces travelers to a spectacular fusion of local customs with Western festive elements. Respect for tradition and formality are critical. When participating in holiday cheer, consider adjusting to local etiquette, such as bowing slightly during greetings in Japan or removing shoes where requested. These small gestures symbolize respect for the culture and reciprocate the warmth often displayed by hosts.

Finally, in the Southern Hemisphere, markets shine under the sun's rays, giving Christmas a unique twist. Australia and New Zealand swap snow for sandy beaches, but the heart of festive celebration remains intact. Here, casual friendliness reigns supreme, and embracing the laid-back nature of locals is key. Engaging in a simple chat about shared love for the season can turn a market visit into a treasured memory.

Whichever corner of the world your Christmas market adventures take you, understanding and honoring cultural etiquettes enriches the journey. These festivities are more than buying handcrafted gifts; they provide a lens into the heart and spirit of a culture at its most joyous time of year. Whether it's through sharing a local delicacy, learning about historical traditions, or simply smiling at a stranger, the Christmas market experience is amplified when approached with cultural sensitivity and openness. Each interaction becomes a spark that contributes to the vibrant mosaic of the global holiday season.

Made in the USA
Columbia, SC
02 December 2024